Dear Volleyball

AbdulAziz Baig

Dear Volleyball

Copyright ©2023 AbdulAziz Baig

ISBN 978-1-7349758-9-5

All rights reserved. No part of this publication may be reproduced, distributed, or transmitted in any form or by any means, including photocopying, recording, or other electronic or mechanical methods, without the prior written permission of the publisher, except in the case of brief quotations embodied in critical reviews and certain other noncommercial uses permitted by copyright law.

Book design by Nan Barnes, StoriesToTellBooks.com

Dear Volleyball

Contents

Dedication	vii
Acknowledgments	viii
1. Where Do I Even Begin?	1
2. It was Love at First Sight	7
3. Our First Time Was a No-Win	20
4. The Second, Not So Bright	32
5. My Time with You Changed Me	43
6. I Was Given a Family	51
7. Moments That Made Me Happy	58
8. Crouched and Ready, I Wait Desperately	63
9. My Heart Fully Committed to You	69
10. I'm So Happy When I'm On the Court	71
11. The Feeling I Get is Always New	81
12. Like the Opening of a Story, So Very Short	87
13. One Can Only Dream	97
14. All We've Been Through	106
15. The Sweeps So Clean	109
16. The Hard-Earned Dues	116
17. In the End, You Kept Me Going	119
18. My Heart and Soul Continually Growing	128
19. From Watching You on the Sidelines	132
20. Dreaming of Victory	141
21. To Holding Up a Trophy of a Lifetime	147
22. Making History	159

23. I Never Wanted It to End	161
24. Times of Joy and Happiness	169
25. The Beautiful Moments with Friends	173
26. Isn't It So Sweet?	187
27. The Next One After	189
28. I Can't Believe We're Here	198
29. At the End of a Chapter	208
30. Ten Letters Spell Volleyball	223
31. You Will Always Be Above All	228
32. Part of the Journey is the End	236
33. To You, My Love and Laughter	240
34. Forever in My Heart, Thank You, My Best Friend	245
35. Dear Volleyball	252
2017-2018 Montgomery Blair High School Coed Volleyball Roster	254

Dedication

This book is dedicated to anyone I've had the pleasure of knowing in my life, but especially to my two coaches, Elliott Shiotani and Jacquieline Armstead-Thomas, to my family and friends, and lastly, to my teammates. I thank you all for being a part of my life. We often think that life is the journey of a single person. Life is so much more. Life is the journey of a single person whose timeline becomes intertwined with others in magical ways.

To Mr. Stelzner, who despite my doubts, gave me hope and helped me become a better writer. With his aid and inspiration, I was able to write this book. We all need teachers in our life. I was lucky to meet one who was not only an excellent role model, but a great friend. I've loved superheroes since I was a kid. As I've gotten older, I now realize that heroes don't just exist in the world of Marvel and DC comics. Sometimes they can be your English teacher. Thank you, Mr. Stelzner, and wherever you are, know you will always be in my heart!

To the sport of volleyball, thank you for the opportunity of a lifetime. I will always love you.

Acknowledgments

It has been two years since my 2017-2018 coed volleyball season, when I first had the idea of writing this book. I could never find the time or right mood to write it, but as I started working on this project, I gained a new perspective and appreciation for the writing process. Like any author will tell you, writing is not easy, but with the help of wonderful people, it can be made much easier and more fruitful. This final version is much more polished than the first draft. I thank everyone who has been a part of this journey and who has contributed to this book in any way.

To Mr. Biff Barnes, I thank you for guiding me on this journey of writing and helping me realize a dream. I wish my thanks could equal what you have done for me, but I could write out my gratitude for pages on end and it still would not be enough. Like the infinite complexities and randomness that add flavor to the beauty of life, I could not foresee just how wondrous of an experience I would have working with you. It has truly been one of the most enriching encounters I have had in my life. Your kindness, passion, and ability to connect with people is something I will forever cherish. To the team at Stories to Tell, I thank you all for your work in helping me fully capture and express this story I had to tell. I pray that you all be showered with the same blessings and joy you have given me on this adventure!

Chapter 1

Where Do I Even Begin?

I woke up early in the morning to the sound of my alarm at six a.m. It was Thursday, May 10, 2018. I had an extra bit of energy that day, and my body seemed more eager to get out of bed than ever before. As I walked past my calendar, my eyes locked onto the giant black circle around that day's date. In it were the words, "PLAYOFF GAME VS SHERWOOD," written in all caps. As I continued with my morning routine, each passing second was a constant reminder. A reminder of what the season had been, everything leading up to that game, and everything on the line. I quickly brushed my teeth and started my morning workout.

There was a different kind of aura about that day. I seemed more motivated and awake than usual. I often got lost in my thoughts and started to think about the future, about moments that hadn't yet occurred, about plays that hadn't even developed. All athletes know this feeling all too well. As I began to walk through my pool of thoughts, I somehow tried to project myself into the future to gain an advantage. I thought maybe, if I tried hard enough, I could see glimpses of what would happen. But no matter how hard I tried, I could not see past what was in front of me. The future was not yet written. The present was still going.

There was a light breeze that morning. I remember seeing the sun begin to rise just behind the trees of the tennis court. Its beams of light pierced through the forest onto the pavement, illuminating the path I was on. That morning had a very calm and serene nature to it. But as I jogged around my neighborhood, I could only think about one word: *Sherwood*. That one word had been on my mind the entire season. Like a constant pain in my heart, it never seemed to go away, returning every second of my life to remind me of my failures, of our failures.

That day started like any other at Montgomery Blair High School, only for us seniors it was different. It was nearing the end of our four-year journey. As I walked from the cafeteria entrance to my first-period class, I could hear bits of conversation about the coming main event. What seemed to occupy the minds of us seniors on the volleyball team was not our imminent graduation or school-related work; rather, it was a brief moment in time that could not only celebrate how far we had come but could come to define who we were to be.

It was very hard to concentrate in class that day, if I'm being honest. As teachers lectured on the various concepts of mathematical principles, history, or the significance of symbols crafted by an author, their voices somehow morphed into pregame pep talks. The sounds of students in the classroom became fans in the bleachers, and the rows of equations written across the whiteboard appeared as if they were X's and O's for a gameplan strategy.

I met Coach Shiotani that day in his room, 233, on the second floor. As always he was sitting at his computer when I walked in, wearing some variation of a flannel shirt, a messy haircut, and devouring a whole bag of candy by himself. Funny enough, he always claimed to have just run out of his candy when I asked him for some. We talked about our game preparations and how we were approaching the rest of our day. His voice seemed to fade away as I lost myself in his eyes. I could see a reflection of my own internal state of being, a deep desire to win and overcome our opponent. It was a desire to solidify our places in history and to leave behind a legacy.

Our conversation into each other's souls was interrupted by teammates and fellow players who joined us for lunch. We all tried our best to mask our nervousness and anxiety, thinking that if we remained quiet, talked about other things, or used humor to deflect anything related to volleyball, it would somehow allow our minds to be elsewhere. But it was clear that we all felt a fearful sense of urgency. Our conversations in our volleyball group chat seemed to only heighten our fears. Our usual talkative nature seemed to fade away. We seemed to be more concerned with what-if scenarios than what was occurring in the present.

It was during my final period that I vividly remember hearing the school-wide announcement system turn on. That was a strange occurrence, given that announcements usually aired in the morning. The front-office representative, who we greeted every morning just as we walked in the front of the school, announced the upcoming volleyball game later that day. The Montgomery Blair High School coed volleyball team was traveling to Sherwood High School to play in a semi-final playoff game, the first in Blair coed-volleyball history. This was a momentous and unique occasion for the school—and rightfully so. Never had any coed volleyball team made it that far into the post-season, and the fact that Sherwood would be at the opposite end of the battle only took the importance of the game to another level. If there was a dynasty every school envied in the county, it was Sherwood. They were always dominant in every sport, winning division titles and county championships year in and year out.

At times I can still hear the sound of the speaker system coming on and the voice of the front-office representative grabbing everyone's attention. Our very own coed volleyball team will be traveling to Sherwood High School later today for a semi-final playoff game. Don't forget to show your Blair pride and come out to show your support for the volleyball team. GO BLAZERS!"

Go Blazers. Those two words kept looping in my head like a tape recorder set to infinitely play a track. Those were words I had heard for four years at least once a day, yet that day they seemed to penetrate deep into my heart and resonate with a true sense of power. The front-office representative, who normally exemplified a calm and cool personality, broke free from her usual self and tapped into her own Blazer pride. Everyone became fired up for the gladiator match that was to come. Those two words were more than just a simple announcement, they were a declaration of pride and honor, and for the first time I could internally understand the significance and responsibility of what it meant to represent my school on such a stage.

At 2:30 the last bell rang and it was finally time. My heart had kicked into high gear and was now beating faster than ever. Each second that passed only seemed to intensify my nerves. The bus would arrive a couple of hours later that evening to take the team to Sherwood, but I had already let the coaches know I was driving there on my own. Normally, our team bus rides were little adventures of their own, often including a mini-concert on the part of everyone screaming at the top of their lungs as we drove down the highway or some debate about any topic that came to mind. But something about the bus ride that day did not feel right to me when it came to preparing mentally before the game. At the time I thought going to the game alone would be the best thing to do to keep my focus. I would not realize it until much later that I would go on to regret that decision for the rest of my life.

I had asked my best friends to accompany me to the game, and they had graciously agreed. It was a long drive from Blair, but the long distance was oddly something I needed. It gave me time to think and really reflect on my experiences in the volleyball program at Blair and as a student in general. As I got lost in my thoughts, a sudden glimpse of blue broke my view.

"We're here," I said as we pulled into the Sherwood parking lot. There were crowds of people outside the school that day, heading into the gym. Parents, students, and fellow athletes were highlighted in their blue uniforms with the word "Warriors" painted proudly across them. Our red colors were a stark contrast and immediately drew the eyes of everyone as we sprinted to the gym. It was like two armies meeting each other on the battlefield, only they had home-court advantage and I was late to the start of it all. Glances were exchanged, and there was a dangerous sense of conflict in the air. I could physically feel the sense of rivalry as I sprinted into the gym through the back entrance.

As I sprung the doors open, I immediately saw a familiar sight: the Sherwood trophy case just outside the gym entrance, a very well-thought-out place to have it if you ask me. Trophies of gold, glittering with pride and success, taunted us as we entered. It was more than just a volleyball playoff game; it was a chance to prove something and take down a goliath.

As I entered the gym, I could already see that the game had started and we were down by five points. I felt my stomach drop when I saw the scoreboard and the faces of my team as I approached them. I quickly sprinted to our bench and could sense the disappointment and shock from everyone. In a state of exhaustion, I tried my best to apologize for being late, but Coach Shiotani simply motioned me with his hand to forget everything and get into the game as quickly as possible. As I subbed in, I felt a deep sense of guilt and shame. I had played with these five people the entire season, yet it seemed as though I had no right to be on the same court with them for that semi-final game. I apologized for my lateness and then focused on the upcoming play. The ref whistled to signal the Sherwood player to proceed with their serve. As contact was made with the ball, I could see it come toward me in slow motion. I took a deep breath, and we were off!

Chapter 2

It was Love at First Sight

Growing up, I was always very active, and from the stories my parents and family related to me, it seemed as though at times I may have been too active. As I walk around my house today and look at many things that are currently broken, be it a picture frame on the wall, an old vase, or some other item that had some sentimental value, I would ask my family what the story was behind it breaking. Initially, they would tell me a story about how my younger cousins and I found some elaborate game that led to something breaking, but now, given how many things I had broken, they just point at me to let me know I had some involvement when I was younger.

My youth was rich with moments of joy and happiness. I remember each part of the house as another extension of my imagination. My cousins and I would recreate the living and dining rooms as our makeshift field or the hallway as our bowling alley. The basement was always the wrestling arena, and practically anything we could think of became our playground. Our love of comic book superheroes or any other science fiction fantasy meant role playing as our favorite heroes and recreating the many iconic moments we grew up watching in our homes.

My family was heavily involved in physical activities and sports throughout the years. Many of my uncles and elders in the family participated in some kind of sport. They all grew up in the Washington, D.C., sports tradition, coming together every Sunday to watch football and even having yearly parties just for the Superbowl. It brought everyone in the whole family together and taught me about the importance and power of sports beyond the act of playing or watching it. I learned it was something that could bring people together to celebrate some of the most precious moments in life.

There were always various types of sports equipment laying around at the house, and at a young age I always played with them, growing a sense of curiosity as to the purpose and rules behind each one. Of course I knew nothing about each sport, but I improvised. The field hockey stick was my at-home lightsaber, frisbees became my makeshift Captain America shields, and just about anything I could find became another tool in my arsenal of superhero powers.

My name is AbdulAziz Baig, but you can call me Aziz. I'm from Silver Spring, a fairly large town in the beautiful state of Maryland. I have been here all my life. Silver Spring is one of the more famous and populated cities in the state. With a population of over 81,000 people, it's a hot spot for people from all over the world. We have our famous downtown Silver Spring, the mecca of our little city. Down the road we have the University of Maryland, College Park. Here you can enjoy all sorts of things, whether you're someone who loves city life or is more of a nature-oriented person. You probably expect me to tell you how amazing this place is, or that it's the best city in the world, but I can't say that. All I know is that this place is home to me, and I can't imagine being anywhere else.

When people ask me about what sport I started playing first, they are shocked to hear it wasn't volleyball. My first ever dip into the world of organized sports came in soccer. My cousin, his younger brother, and I played together one season for a youth soccer league in the local area. Although it was only for a year, it was an amazing experience and a really successful year for us. We secured an undefeated record and made it all the way to the finals, only to lose very badly to a team we had beaten earlier that same year. I remember feeling so angry at myself about how I played, and still to this day that loss has not left me.

Although it was not the ending I wanted, it was an important learning experience for me. I learned not only a great deal about my own abilities, I also learned about winning and losing and all the other things that come with being an athlete, like how to be part of a team and to have fun with whatever it is you are doing. Many of my soccer skills would even make it onto the court during volleyball games too, so that was a big help as well!

It's sort of weird looking back to that first time when I fell in love with volleyball, but it still lingers in the back of my mind as if it were only yesterday. Prior to volleyball, I could never find it in me to fully love a sport. I enjoyed watching and playing various sports for fun, but I never really committed to one sport; that is, until I found volleyball for the first time.

I remember years ago scavenging through some old things in the attic one day and finding a strange white orb sitting in the back behind some large boxes. It had a clear glow to it as it stood out among everything around it. Like a celestial body, its gravitational pull drew me closer until I was in its orbit. As I turned it around, I saw an odd image on it, a red painting of a face. It was striped weirdly with zippered lines running around in an organized manner. I would later come to find out that my uncle happened to have the same volleyball as the one in that Tom Hanks movie Castaway. You know, the one where he yells the name of that volleyball.

I remember being perplexed about it. Being so young, I had no idea what it was, given I had only experienced a handful of sports. It was strange holding it for the first time. It didn't feel familiar. I knew it wasn't a basketball because they had a rubber-type feel to them and were usually orange. It was light and smooth to the touch, whereas soccer balls were much heavier, and it certainly wasn't a football.

I took it outside and began to play around with it a little. Throwing it in the air, bouncing it on the ground and off the walls. I even tried hitting it up and down with my palm to no success. My uncle saw me from a distance and laughed a little. He called me over and asked what I was doing. I told him I just happened to find this ball in the house. He asked if I knew what it was and I told him I didn't. That was the first time I heard the word "volleyball." *What the heck is volleyball?* I instantly became hooked. He told me what the sport was and how it was played. I don't remember feeling super excited. At the time it was just another sport I was learning about, but that moment in time would go on to change the rest of my life in a significant way.

—∞—

As a family we would take a yearly trip to the beach at Sandy Point State Park in Annapolis, Maryland. That year, I had decided to bring Wilson along and began playing the sport. I grew really close to the sport in a short span of time. I practiced by myself, but I wasn't doing any good. I couldn't seem to get my arms in the right position to pass the ball, and because I was so used to other sports, and the usual motion of throwing or kicking a ball, it felt like learning how to walk again. I could get up maybe one pass, and that was it before it shot off, hitting someone's car parked out front.

Something about learning volleyball was very artistic, and I could never understand why. Usually in sports, you have control over whatever it is you're doing, but with volleyball it was different. It felt like the ball had some weird control over me. It forced me to sort of forget what I knew about sports and approach learning in a new way. There is an interesting relationship between a volleyball player and a volleyball. Each sport is like a language, and I was just getting my introduction to Volleyball 101.

In a way, a volleyball has a mind of its own. You can guide it, but it does what it wants, and it was tough in the beginning. I practiced for hours and still couldn't manage to get better. In the world of sports, what's often advertised or perpetuated is the idea that in order to learn something or to master something, you need to just focus on getting stronger or faster. But in volleyball that isn't really the case. All who've played it know it requires a total balance of mind and body. It isn't so much about how strong you are as it is how disciplined you are. The sport requires you to humble yourself and relax. It tests your patience and composure. Each time you interact with a volleyball, it is speaking directly to you. You can either ignore what it's saying and try to control the conversation, or you can allow it to speak to your heart and guide you.

On our yearly trips to the beach, we would have a competitive family volleyball game on the sand courts, at least 10 people on either side. At the time I was sure that wasn't how it actually was supposed to be, but it was fun, nonetheless. Of course, we didn't play the sport the real way. There weren't any real rotations or lineups, not even any positions, really. The rules were basically to make sure the ball didn't touch down on your side of the court and do whatever you could to get it on the other side. It was so thrilling to play, despite the lack of rules. It brought out something in me that other sports could not parallel. It awakened a passion and love for the game that I never had with any other sport. That's when I knew volleyball was it for me.

At my private school in College Park, volleyball wasn't a popular sport; in fact, it was nonexistent. Especially when it came to men playing volleyball, there were always stereotypes or teasing for any guy who played volleyball or even spoke of it. Things like football or soccer were always popular, but I never could find that yearning desire to commit to those sports. I often practiced volleyball at home on a wall or passed to myself, given I had no one to play with or any clubs to play for. Those hours spent alone were pretty extraordinary, transformative, and even meditative in some way. I had time to myself, and I could always think about nothing else and just enjoy having a fun time wherever I practiced.

I watched games wherever and whenever I could, and it only increased my love for the sport. I always had questions about why players were standing a certain way and why they did different things in different situations. I remember noticing how every team had one specific player who would always get the second pass and that after each point, the teams would rotate. I did my research about the sport and learned about the basic rules and formalities of how to approach the game. Things like how the sport evolved over time and how the game is actually played. I was shocked when I learned that it was a 6 vs 6 game, unlike our 10-man teams! I also learned about positions, like the setter and libero. I have always found libero to be an interesting word. *Libero. Where did that ever come from?* My desire to learn about volleyball became an obsession to a certain degree.

With other sports, so much is required from a physical point of view. Your body has to be fit and ready to withstand forces like running or contact, but in volleyball you don't directly interact with opposing players. Although you still need to maintain physical fitness, it's a more mental and holistic sport. I had to change the way I approached practicing and playing it because I was so used to growing up watching sports that were completely the other way around.

I vividly remember once playing on the beach years after first learning about volleyball. It had seemed as though there were times when everything around me seemed to slow down on the court. As I made contact with the ball, I could calculate things happening around me in mere seconds, whether it was where the other players were on the court and in relation to me or what play to execute. Although it lasted only a few seconds, I could sense there was something about this sport I had yet to discover. Something about the sport forces you to become an artist of sorts. You have to use all your senses to create a work of art. Just like when an artist has a blank canvas and they have to decide what their plan is before they can execute it. At times things happen along the way that don't follow an organized or preplanned outline, yet it is as if you are being guided by something more than yourself. In volleyball, similarly, every point is a blank canvas, and there is a certain level of conscious effort toward making a play happen. Still, there is also an aura about the sport that cannot be explained or even controlled. You just know it's happening when you are in the moment, and when it all comes together, the play is picture perfect.

As the years went on, I started to up my game by the day. I began watching college and international volleyball a lot. I enjoyed the level of play various players showed with their hard-hitting and rocket-speed jump serves, and I tried to study players in different positions. I didn't gravitate to any one position in particular. Being a setter was cool because it meant you were always involved for the most part in every play, and you were the center of the team, but I wasn't very good at it. The ball would always slip through my hands or spin really fast, which meant I would likely be called for many doubles. (A double is when a player makes more than one contact on a ball, which is a likely occurrence for inexperienced setters.) It also looked really hard. You were always running around the court, and all the pressure was on you. Playing in the middle was fun, but I wasn't that tall, which meant players would likely hit over me with ease. And even if I could play, I wouldn't be able to go back row, which meant no passing.

Hitting and passing were what I gravitated toward, and the outside and right-side hitting positions (left and right front) were where I wanted to be. The do-it-all nature of those positions caught my eye. I loved how hitters could instill their position and will on opposing defenses in a multitude of ways. As a hitter you have free range to execute where and how you want to hit a ball, and that sort of guessing game you play with the defense was very intriguing. I loved watching plays where a hitter would jump for a full-swing play and then all of a sudden throw a smokescreen and end up tipping or rolling the ball for an easy point. Of course, the hitting part was cool, too! There is no feeling like spiking a ball directly between defenses and seeing their shocked and disappointed faces.

Passing was absolutely mesmerizing to me. Passing requires a certain level of grace on the court. As I watched players on the court easily dig up hits, I saw they had a smooth aura about themselves. They never seemed to worry about their opponents, and they made it look easy as they maneuvered the court and executed perfect passes that led to perfect sets. Passers also had to be ready for anything, and that mystery behind guessing where opposing hitters were going to target made me fall in love with that aspect of defense. I would come to realize later on that passing was anything but easy!

I always wanted to play on a team, but with my schedule at private school, I could never find time to play. Our private school didn't have any sports, and no one I knew played volleyball. It wasn't until I transferred to a public high school that I first joined a sport in a competitive fashion.

Montgomery Blair High School, located at the intersection of University Boulevard and Colesville Road, was a fairly new school. The old Blair was located a couple of minutes away, where Silver Spring International Middle School now stands. I grew up loving Blair, not only because it was right next to where I lived but because I grew up with the Blair tradition. Many people from my family attended Blair, and I even went to many games when I was a kid. Every Friday I would hear the announcer during football games on the main field and hear the sounds of hundreds of fans cheering on their fellow Blazers.

I had never gone to a public school before Blair, which meant I had to learn everything about public-school life and make new friends. Education for me was in a private school all my life until eighth grade. It was extremely religious and gender-segregated, too. Boys on one side, girls on the other, so I never knew what it was like going to school in a different environment. We also wore the same outfit combination for all the years I was there: a white polo with blue slacks. Can you believe we wore the same outfit for nine years? That was something I didn't miss.

There were things, however, that I did miss when I transferred to Blair. I missed all my old friends and teachers. I missed not ever having to worry about college or responsibilities. At private school, I could go to school knowing I would have a great time with people I had known pretty much all my life. Leaving all that behind was pretty tough. I remember telling my friends about it. Their expressions were enough for me to understand what they felt. Things would never be the same, but I guess life is all about change. I sure wish it wasn't. I wish we didn't have to grow up. I wish we could play all the time like we did as kids.

Telling my parents about the whole public-school thing was a whole other story. I finally mustered up enough courage to speak to my parents about transferring to a public school. What had populated my life for nine years was now suddenly out of my sight, and I was nervous about asking. They were pretty strict about the whole religious thing, but that wasn't my concern; I wouldn't have to worry about that. But I had started to wonder about my future and things like going to college.

I didn't know how my parents were going to react, but after long hours of talk, they finally gave in. I knew I wanted to go to Blair all along. Oddly enough, something happened and I was put in another high school even though I lived right behind Blair. I remember being torn about that. It felt like that dream you've always had was now being crushed. We tried again and again and, after much convincing, were able to get the school we picked. I look back at that moment and wonder how different my life would be had I not gone to Blair.

In my freshman year at Blair, I played junior varsity football. It was what all my cousins and family had played and loved, so I did it, but something about it was off. I never seemed to have that feeling of wanting to play football. Football was a passion for me to watch and play but only ever in a non-organized context. My first year happened to also be a terrible year for JV, as we only won a couple of games and were blown out of the rest. During our season opener against Sherwood High School, we lost by over 40 points to 0, and to make it worse, my entire family had come to watch. The scheduling of it was also extremely difficult. After school we had an hour for what was referred to as study hall, a time for players to do schoolwork, but it was spent mostly having fun with friends and doing anything but schoolwork.

Football practice began after study hall and lasted for about two hours. They were difficult and exhausting hours, given the intense heat. Wearing pads was always uncomfortable, and our practices were always extended. We ran constantly after practice, and by the end of the day, I was so exhausted that I had no energy to do schoolwork. I would come home from practice, often walking, and go directly to sleep. Waking up a couple of hours before school the next morning, I would finish whatever work I could and finish the rest during lunch. That was what every day was like for the entire season. By the end of it, I had serious doubts about returning and, ultimately, decided toward the end of my freshman year to leave football, which wasn't easy. Over the season I had created a bond with the head coach, and he wasn't too pleased abouth me leaving. I had also grown close to many of my teammates, whom I'm still close to until this day, but I knew in the end that football was not for me.

I remained uncertain during the spring semester that school year. Although I did not miss the many difficult aspects of football, there were times when I deeply missed other things, such as Thursday practices without pads or spending time with friends heading to the shopping center near Blair. I would walk home sometimes only to pass by the school gym or the practice field and hear the familiar sounds which I had grown accustomed to only months prior. I did, however, gain a new sense of appreciation for that year of football. Although it wasn't a successful season, it taught me a great deal about sports and everything that is required of you. Being an athlete is its own unique journey, but being a student athlete in high school and having to juggle various aspects of your identity and life is a truly unique experience. With football I was able to understand what it meant to truly be a student athlete, that it is not only about the good things but also about the tough experiences, both of which blend together and shape who you are.

It also gave me a new appreciation for life. There are many parallels to life that can be drawn from sports, and from that point on, my views on sports completely changed. Although a part of me missed hearing the familiar sounds and voices of football, I knew I had to move on. I had looked at other sports to try out for, but none of them really caught my eye. That same spring semester of my freshman year, I had the opportunity to play another sport, but football had drained a love for playing organized sports out of me and I needed some time away to reset.

In my sophomore year of high school, an announcement was made about volleyball tryouts. I remember my eyes lighting up when I heard those words because it had never occurred to me that Blair had a volleyball team. I decided to learn about the program and see if it was something I could be interested in. Walking into the room where the information meeting was held started the adventure of a lifetime for me; however, I was not aware of it at the time.

Volleyball would soon become my life. It was something I could always turn to. Even as I laid in bed, I could mentally set the ball for hours and not have to worry about anything going on outside. Volleyball is a very peaceful sport. There isn't any need for over-aggressiveness or anger. It's more about keeping yourself in a peaceful state to play at an optimum level. Even now, as I continue to play years later, I still get the same tingles on the court I did when I first found volleyball. That's what I love about it so much. Despite how many times I go back to it, somehow it's like I'm playing it for the first time. I knew in an instant that volleyball was love at first sight.

Chapter 3

Our First Time Was a No-Win

At the end of August right before the start of my sophomore year, I recall being in my room, doubting my decision to leave football. When I was playing football, I had a great time learning about practice, meeting new people, and getting to know what life was like as an athlete. It had been on my mind for a while that I wanted to rejoin the team. It was tough, I must admit. I spoke to people I knew about the decision, and ultimately, I had to find comfort in not playing it anymore.

My sophomore year felt strange that first semester. Not having a sport after school was really boring. All I did was go home right after my final period, do homework, and catch one of my favorite TV shows or movies. One day I happened to hear something about volleyball tryouts from a friend in my math class. They spoke about how amazing it was to create lasting memories with teammates and the joys of playing a sport together. I wanted to have those same experiences as well. What made me hesitant was that I had never played volleyball on a team before, but I thought it couldn't be as bad as football. Volleyball was played during the spring semester, giving me enough time to think about my decision.

The spring sports announcement made by the front-office representative, stated there would be an informational meeting on the second floor in room 233. Each year the school had announcements in advance about upcoming sports tryouts or meetings, but this one was unusually early. After school I decided to stop by days earlier than what the announcement had said because I knew it would be less anxiety-provoking to go in and not have to worry about being a stranger in a new crowd.

I walked in, and right in front of me was a computer screen. Behind it was some teacher I had never seen or met. He wore a flannel shirt and was fixated on whatever he was doing. I politely got his attention and asked if this was the right place for a volleyball meeting. Of course I knew it was the right room, but I was so nervous that I didn't know what else to say. The teacher introduced himself as Elliott Shiotani. He had been hired as the coed volleyball coach for the 2015-2016 season after the previous coach left. He was very kind and handed me some paperwork as well as some information about the sport. I thanked him and walked out. He seemed like a cool person, but I still had my doubts about playing.

However, the thought of playing volleyball stuck with me every day after meeting Coach Shiotani. It didn't matter what I was doing or thinking about, somehow, my mind always went back to volleyball. I went back and forth about what I should do, and there were times I felt like not playing. It wasn't so much about not liking it or anything like that; I was just really nervous. I was still fresh in the public school system and adjusting to things, and I had never played volleyball in an organized way.

One day during PE we happened to play volleyball as part of the net-sports requirement for the class. My cousin was also there as well as a mutual friend we had made in class. As we played with each other, we noticed how committed we were to the game. Normally, students didn't take sports seriously, but we took this game of ours seriously, and our mutual friend noticed. For some odd reason the upcoming season came up in conversation. Like my cousin and me, he had heard about the announcement for spring sports and asked if we were planning to try out for anything. I wasn't sure at the time, so I gave him the usual "I don't know" answer. He said he was trying out for coed volleyball and that we should also join.

All the signs were pointing me in the direction of playing, but I still couldn't go through with it. To sort of ease my mind and get some guidance on what to do, I decided to discuss it with Coach Shiotani. That same day after school, I walked into his office, and there he was again, wearing his flannel shirt.

God, does he love wearing flannels. I asked him more about his background and the sport itself. Funny enough, I discovered he had never played or coached volleyball in his life. He was the varsity field hockey head coach at Blair during the fall semester and knew nothing about the sport of volleyball other than the fact that, "It was a sport where you hit a ball," as he put it.

At that point the obvious thing to do would have been to just thank him and walk away. That had to be the sign I was looking for. There was no way I was going to play for someone who had never coached or played. But something about him felt relatable. He went on about how the school hadn't had a coach for this season. The athletic director had put the word out about looking for someone to volunteer as a coach, and Shiotani happened to accept the offer, given he didn't coach during the spring season. He said he wanted to try something new, and volleyball would allow him to learn about a new sport he had never really paid much attention to.

I can still vividly picture his round face and his black hair in a comb-over messy look. He spoke with a weird accent, and at times I giggled at the way he pronounced certain words, like "outside." (Sorry, Shio!) But when I looked into his eyes that day, I felt he was after something more than just coaching a sport he had never previously given a second thought to. I couldn't accept his statement about wanting to join volleyball just for fun. There had to be some catch that I couldn't see at the time. It was one of those magical instances you have in life where things sort of lined up, and I knew at that moment that I needed to play for him.

—⚃—

Montgomery Blair High School was a laughing stock when it came to coed volleyball, and that's an understatement. The school had never accomplished anything and had maintained a consistent losing record year after year. It was effectively a ghost sport at the school. They had those odd years where they were good, but in its entire history, Blair had never won a division title or county championship. In volleyball, not even qualifying for playoffs is an indication of how bad a team is, given how many teams make the playoffs in the county.

My freshman year, the 2014-2015 season, was by all accounts the best season for any Blair coed volleyball team in history to that date. They had made the playoffs for the first time after years of a playoff drought, securing a 7-4 record as well as locking up a 4-1 record, which placed them second in their division. They were eliminated early in the first round of the playoffs and the team had broken up, the girls mostly graduating or leaving for their club teams during the spring season and the boys leaving for the varsity boys team. There was no foundation and there weren't many expectations for the sport. It sort of became a sport people joined just to say they were on a team at Blair.

I was heartbroken at the reputation the sport had at Blair, along with how people perceived it, which was not only limited to Blair. In a country dominated by sports like football and basketball, people often never get to see how amazing and wonderful other sports are.

I loved volleyball so much, and it broke my heart that coed, in particular, became a sport no one at the school cared about. I wanted to change that. I told myself that if I couldn't win anything, at least I could help change the culture and perception of the sport at the school in the hopes that somehow the future would be more promising than the present.

My first year playing volleyball—the 2015-2016 season—was a terrible year by every account. Not only was it a trial year for Coach Shio, as he was learning the ins and outs of volleyball while simultaneously trying to coach it, but no one really knew much about the sport itself. A good majority of the team were first-year players like me, so we spent much of our time just trying to get on par with learning the basics of how to actually play volleyball.

Tryouts began in a small gym that was shared by both the varsity boys and the coed teams. It only added to how much—or how little—the school cared about the sport. It was obvious that they gave other sports preferences over volleyball. I didn't blame them; anyone would have done the same. Given the limited space, drills had to be run by the coed and varsity boys teams together on one net.

Walking into that gym for the first time was nerve wracking, to say the least. My entire body trembled with fear, so much so that I thought about leaving at one point, but I had come this far and had to at least try. I remember doing poorly on everything. I couldn't serve, pass, or hit. I was playing scared every chance I had. Playing volleyball is fun on the beach when you're with your family, but when you have two coaches in a room, watching your every move, and you're surrounded by people who've played for years, you get a little nervous, given how terrible you look compared to them. All I could think about was whether or not I was going to make the team.

During one of the hitting drills, I approached the set and timed it a little too late. The ball hit the net and fell directly at my feet. Feeling dejected, I picked it up with my head down and jogged over to the other hitting line. As I was walking, I heard a voice call me over. It was the coach of the varsity boys team. He had been coaching at Blair forever, sort of solidifying himself as a volleyball legend at the school. I walked over with a nervous look on my face, expecting harsh criticism and disappointment. He looked me in the eyes and, with his words of encouragement and a smile, calmed me down. He introduced himself as Chris Liang.

"First time playing?" he asked.

I nodded my head slowly.

"Don't worry too much about it. When I first played, I was terrible, much worse than you, if you can believe it. Go out there and do your best, stop worrying about being perfect, and do whatever you can."

I was shocked. Here he was, someone I had never met before, giving me some advice and a little confidence. It was nice to hear those words. It was like having someone put their arm around you and tell you everything was going to be okay. If it weren't for that, I don't know how I would have made it through that first tryout. From that point

Coach Chris

on, tryouts became a little easier. I felt my body relax more, and I stopped worrying about the tryout part and just played volleyball to the best of my abilities.

There were three consecutive days of tryouts, each with increasing anxiety about making the team. Luckily, I made the cut, even with my poor performance. *There is no way I should have made the cut, given how I played*, I thought, but to my surprise I found out that everyone who tried out for the team made it. I guess that's how coed volleyball was at Blair.

Despite the culture surrounding the sport, I was super excited, nonetheless, to finally be on a team and have the opportunity to play a sport I loved. My cousin was also on the team, along with our mutual friend from PE whom we had known for a while. That was nice because it meant I wouldn't be a complete stranger on the team. I also knew some people from class, so fitting in wouldn't be a problem.

Our team was a squad of players that I can only describe as if you had closed your eyes and pointed at random people in a crowd to join the team. There were a handful of players who had experience playing, but it was never enough to lift our team to the status of a qualified unit.

Despite our lack of skills or any type of actual talent, we still endured and practiced for weeks heading into the season. I must admit that practices were fun and exciting as we inched our way closer to the season opener. With the amount of energy and excitement we had going into that season, one would have thought we were bound to win the county championship. That was anything *but* what happened that year. With our newly bound team and fresh introduction to volleyball, we managed to somehow pull away with two miraculous wins for the season and go 2-9. Our two wins came against Einstein and Bethesda-Chevy Chase High School; like us, they were also in a rebuild mode. Even with the cluster of bad teams that year, we didn't even qualify for the low playoff spots in the county, only further proving how bad we were. Most of our losses were in straight sets, meaning 3-0 defeats. Of the games we did win, none were straight sets. The way our team was structured was not well suited for volleyball. Every team in the county had players uniquely suited for every position. We did not.

At one point toward the end of the year, we had a shot to qualify for a final sport in the playoffs by winning our final game of the season. We traveled about an hour away from school to play a game at Poolesville High School, which is what I can only describe as somewhere in the middle of nowhere. It was a dreadful ride, given how cramped and uncomfortable the bus was, not to mention our preexisting knowledge about how good Poolesville was.

The game occurred on May 2, 2016. Our hopes for a playoff spot are what ultimately kept us alive on the ride to the game, but it was to no effect. I remember arriving at this very beautiful campus with lots of greenery all around. The gym ceiling was fairly low compared to ours, but what caught our eyes was the team and the walls littered with accomplishments of the school's athletic programs. There were county and division championships left and right for various sports, including volleyball. We watched as they practiced on the court. They had their music playing very loudly and were working on hitting lines. Every couple of seconds I would hear the sound of another loud bang, which meant they were not just hitting in but hitting their balls hard. As we sat on our side, watching the boys varsity teams play first, we had an overall sense of fear. We had come a long way from where we started, but we still were not that good.

Playing our hearts out, we tried to keep up with the opposing team, but we could do nothing better than them—except for making mistakes. Poolesville went up two sets very quickly. We poured everything we had into the third set, sprinting across the court, diving, and doing just about everything we could to salvage any points we could. We were lucky to win the third set. The fourth did not feel the same. Poolesville quickly corrected their mistakes and handed us a 3-1 loss. It got so bad that our team started to collapse on itself. We all grew frustrated with how the game was turning out and it all ended on a bad note toward the end of the game. Luckily, Shio somehow pulled us in together and we embraced each other. He reminded us that despite our season, we should be proud of the fact that we fought and never gave up and that he himself had a fun year learning and growing, just like everyone else. We took our final team pictures and left.

The ride home that day after the final game of my first year was very odd. As I look back, I remember looking out the window, and a strange sense of calm overtook me. I tried to put a pin on it, but I couldn't figure out what it was. My first thoughts were that maybe it was just the fact that the season was ending, and all the losing would end, but as I look back on that ride, it finally hit me years later. Although our season was not great, it was still an amazing adventure. It sounds weird, I know, but I often look back at that season and ask myself, if it had happened any other way, would it all have played out the same? Hypothetically, if we had made the playoffs, given our talent, and ended up losing, would it have affected the future? Had we not had that year to learn with the many mistakes we had and the many losses, would we have progressed to where we ended up?

A strange thing about life is that you can try to formulate an infinite number of what-if scenarios, but what you'll find is that none will ever be enough to reach a satisfactory point. The events that have occurred become fully cemented in a carefully crafted timeline, and nothing will change them. That year was very important, not only for Blair volleyball, but for me personally, along with everyone involved. I just didn't know it at the time.

It was a rough year, full of ups and downs—mostly downs—but still, there were parts of the season that were fun. I had such a blast because I was finally enjoying the sport I loved, and practices were always something I could look forward to because we were starting to bond with each other. My smiles would soon begin to fade after the season as I would be reminded of the still-present perceptions about the sport and our 2-9 record. Volleyball was still a joke at Blair, and it wasn't going anywhere.

That first year Blair held its usual spring pep rally on the football field. The whole school watched as sports of all kinds ran out onto the field to celebrate and cheer each other on. I recall the nerves the entire volleyball team had as we gathered at the field entrance. Given how bad our record was, we were afraid of how embarrassing it might be to walk out in front of the whole school. But our record was not mentioned. It was one of those highlights of the year where, despite all the losses, we could smile at each other and enjoy an amazing moment as a team together.

That year Blair also held its first-ever sports awards ceremony in the cafeteria. Normally, sports would assign their team awards individually on their own time. It was customary to do such a thing at banquets outside the school, but Blair wanted to make it an official ceremony where coaches and teams would be recognized for their seasons in front of the whole school. Walking into the cafeteria, which was packed with students and teachers, was nerve wracking because I knew coed had a bad record, and there was a possibility that our record was going to be shown.

I remember how embarrassed I was walking on stage to represent Blair coed volleyball. We all lined up at the center of the stage and were the center of everyone's attention. I turned around to see our season summary on a projected screen and breathed a sigh of relief when I saw no record was posted. I had won the offensive MVP award that year, but I didn't care. It was like accepting a participation award. Every second holding that trophy was a constant reminder of the season. From that day until the start of the next season, all I could think about was how much of a disappointment the season was and, more importantly, how much of a disappointment I was.

We lost crucial pieces on our team that year. A handful of players graduated or left the program along with our most crucial piece, Christine, our setter and captain, who also graduated. Christine was not just our setter and leader; she was the single biggest reason coed had greatly improved over the years. There were times during the year when she was peppered with questions from most of the team during games. I would get lost during games and not know where I was supposed to be and whisper to her, asking her where I should be in various rotations. She graciously and patiently answered all of our questions and played the hardest of anyone on the team.

My cousin left to run track, and it was like being back at square one again, only much worse—if such a thing were even possible. Other players decided to not return that year. I didn't blame them for that decision. Who would want to return to repeat another losing record? Yeah, it was fun to hang out with friends and have a good time during the season, but there is no feeling like winning.

There were times during the summer when I thought about leaving coed and joining the varsity boys team. They had a much stronger team, and Coach Chris and I had grown closer throughout the year. He asked about my interest in joining the boys team, but I put it off, given I was still undecided.

As I sat one day in my room, doing some film studying, for some reason I was reminded of a conversation I'd had with Coach Shiotani before the season started. Because I had been elected captain, we had a one-on-one about expectations and such, the usual formal outlines of rules and guidelines from coach to captain. I remember that, after our conversation, I looked at Shio with a laser-like glare and made him a promise that I vowed would happen before I left coed volleyball.

Chapter 4

The Second, Not So Bright

The summer before the 2016-2017 season, I had nights when I contemplated leaving coed. I would often ask myself whether I had made the right decision to join coed and whether I should play the coming year. I would always hear Coach Chris' voice in my head with his offer to join boys varsity. It was tempting, I must admit. They had a really strong program, and Chris recruited well and developed his players very quickly. The boys team that year was strong, with returning starters who were experienced, and they had a shot at winning both divisions and making a serious run in the playoffs. It took a great toll on me, but I eventually decided to try out for boys varsity.

The mistake I made was not telling Coach Shiotani about it. I sort of just didn't show up for coed tryouts. I still feel a great deal of guilt for choosing to go about it that way, but thankfully, he was cool about it and, in his typical Shio manner, still made me smile and encouraged me to do my best. But I could tell it was on his mind the whole time after I told him.

Tryouts that year were separated now that we had the whole gym back. Boys varsity was on the main side and coed on the other. It was tough on me. I felt like I was betraying my team—which I was. Overall, the drills were much better than the previous year. I had a year of experience under my belt, playing in an organized setting, and I was much more comfortable on the court. I could recognize plays, and the schematic aspects of the game felt more natural and intuitive to me.

Coach Chris, having played and coached the sport most of his life, knew how to adhere to each player and work on their individual level of skill. He gave me a lot of insight into the mental and foundational aspects of the game. I always trained hard with my physical body and dieting, but he always drove the point that those things can only take you so far. The mental aspect of the game is the difficult part, but if you can learn to master it, your game will elevate to new heights.

As tryouts went on, I couldn't concentrate much on whatever was happening in front of me. As I peppered with another player or tried to prepare myself before a ball came my way, I would be distracted by the noise from the coed side. If I happened to look over, I would see my old teammates, along with Coach Shio. It felt strange, being so distant from them. Even though I knew some of the boys varsity players well from the previous year, I wasn't close to them like I was to the coed players.

As a player in any team sport, you develop a close bond with your teammates over the course of season, and that always transcends the sport itself. The coed team we had stuck together through a 2-9 season, and our friendship was what kept us going through it all.

Thoughts of doubt began to cloud my mind again. *What the heck am I doing?* I kept telling myself I shouldn't be on the boys side, I should be with the coed team. I had made a promise to Shio, and I wasn't going to be satisfied until I came through with it. I kindly asked Coach Chris if he would allow me to switch over to coed. As he stood there, slightly bent over with a bottle of soda in his hand, wearing his usual loose clothing and hair slicked over, he graciously allowed me to switch. Thankfully, it was the first day of tryouts, so it wasn't a big deal, although I could tell by his reaction that he was slightly ticked off, given that the depth he had on the boys team was now slightly lessened.

As I walked over to the coed side, faces began to brighten. Frowns turned to smiles as I was greeted with open arms by my old teammates and Shio. It felt like returning home after being overseas for a long vacation. Coed was home for me, and I did not want to be anywhere else. I couldn't go further without those people in my life. With the biggest of smiles, I quickly scanned my immediate surroundings, seeing familiar faces and new ones, too.

The first person who stood out to me was a tall girl with blonde hair standing in the back of the crowd. She was hands down the tallest person on our team other than Brenna, but I already knew Brenna, so it couldn't be her. She introduced herself as Olivia Freer. She had a childlike personality, said she had played on the girl's team, and was an avid volleyball player, participating not only in high school volleyball but club volleyball as well.

I continued to scan the crowd and saw familiar faces of players from the previous year. Joanne, an excellent defensive specialist and deadly server, was a returning starter.

I saw fresh faces as well.

Elisabeth Jang was a new player from girls' volleyball along with many others who had joined coed for the first time. I thought I was finished counting everyone, but then I realized I didn't know who our setter was.

After the 2015-2016 season, we lost Christine when she graduated. I turned and saw this girl walk over. I remembered seeing her once in the gym during practice my first year. It had been during one of our usual drills, and the gym doors opened and out came this girl who approached Shio and had a short chat with him before leaving.

As I snapped back to the present, I refocused my attention on our new setter. She had her black hair tied up in a ponytail, and she wore a half-sleeve shirt. She looked extremely tired, as she had just finished setting drills near the net with someone I also had not met before. "Hi, my name is Jaya," she said. Jaya was also an experienced volleyball player who had played on the girls' varsity team.

Shio walked over, along with another person I didn't recognize. The woman had a clipboard in her hand and was a stark contrast to the relaxed aura of Shio. There was a certain seriousness about her. Shio introduced everyone to Coach Armstead, who was joining the team that year as a coaching assistant. She had volleyball experience, having played throughout her life, and she was to add another dimension to the team to help out Shio with the more scheme-oriented things like lineups or rotations and such. There were many more people, but introductions were over and tryouts resumed.

Drills were much better than the 2015-2016 season. Players who returned had increased their level of play, and the newcomers were either already playing for other teams or were catching on quickly. Having played with each other for a year, the returners found communication much easier, given we knew each other's playing styles. I knew it was a drastic improvement from the previous year, but preseason diagnostics don't tell you anything. *Playing* volleyball tells you *everything*.

Tryouts lasted three days. Given how many people actually showed up, cuts were made, unlike the previous year. I was happy about that. For once, a small gathering was growing for coed volleyball. Word had spread and students had showed up to try out. It wasn't something glamorous, or as much as I had hoped for, but it was a good starting point. I remember that, after the third day, I was in the locker room with some teammates, and we happened to bring up our thoughts about cuts. I, of course, gave the same old "I did my best" talk, but in reality I was genuinely anxious. Although I was returning from the previous year and knew Shio, I was still worried because anything could happen. With a confused look from Shio, I breathed a sigh of relief after he told me I made the team.

Our first Monday practice was the week after tryouts week. Coaches Shiotani and Armstead spared no time in getting that team on a head start. I loved that. Now we were taking this volleyball thing more seriously. There was no more joking around or excuses about being a first-year player. We practiced for two to three hours a day ahead of the season opener. I remember feeling really excited. Practices were going well. Our serving was efficient. Hitting was bolstered now that we had Olivia. Jaya was an excellent setter who really took the position over and became a leader on and off the court. Passing significantly improved with experience, and with the addition of more expert defensive specialists like Elisabeth, we greatly improved on our weaknesses from the previous year. We were only days away from of our first game when the coaches pulled us aside for a talk.

"Okay, everyone, we have to decide on captains for the season," said Shio.

Although picking captains was not something we cared a great deal about, Shio made a point that it was crucial that we get the right captains, not only to set the tone for the team but also to convey expected standards of how we carried ourselves on and off the court. During my first year, picking captains was not taken seriously, and it had reflected on our demeanor as a team. Christine, our senior captain that first year, was among a few who really took the role seriously, whereas, at the time, I did not fully understand the responsibility and role of being a captain.

Captains are more than just leaders, they are an extension of the coaches, and more importantly, they are individuals who players could relate to on a more personal level. Because the coaches can only go so far in terms of how they can reach a player, it is up to captains to have that student-to-student, friend-to-friend bond with other players. I would only later come to find out how important that was.

We floated names around. Jaya was the obvious first choice. She was both a setter and an experienced player at Blair. Other names were thrown for a second. Brenna was also another experienced player and was the pillar of our team, both on the court as a middle and off the court as a natural-born leader, making her the perfect choice for co-captain. Coaches Shio and Armstead wanted an extra captain that year, given the increase in the overall number of players on the team. Olivia's name was thrown out there, but she was only a freshman. Other names were mentioned but they were also very inexperienced and underclassmen.

I can still picture the next moment in my head. Shio turned to me and said, "Aziz, you're a captain again."

I could hear from the tone of his voice that there was no hesitation or second guessing. His decision was final. I didn't know why he chose me, but I trusted his judgment. I had been chosen captain my first year, but that was because there really wasn't anyone else who wanted it. I tended to shy away from being a captain, but Shio would later show me why it was an important position.

―∞―

The 2016-2017 season was a great improvement from the previous year. We played with much more flow and comfort within the game. We won four games, which wasn't that much of an increase, but the improvements in the team were drastic. It wasn't so much that we won more games as it was building on what we had done the previous season. Another important element of that year was that we were finally starting to create a true foundation for coed volleyball. Our wins came against Richard Montgomery, Einstein, Kennedy, and Northwood. Three of those wins came against division opponents (Einstein, Kennedy, and Northwood), which was a great boost to morale as well.

A culture change had to start somewhere. Most of the players on the team were young and only underclassmen, so they could develop and continue to grow as well as carry the momentum for years to come. With our record we secured a spot in the playoffs, but our low record meant we had to play the elite teams in the county. Because of how the county system works, you have the highest-seeded team playing with the lowest-seeded team, working its way to the middle (first place versus last place, second place versus second last place, and so on). Our record had us facing off against the third-ranked team in the county.

Shio was very excited to be coaching in his first-ever playoff game, as was I. It felt surreal to make it past the regular season and see how much progress we had made thus far. Other players were confused by our excitement, but they were unaware of the prior years of coed, so they didn't understand the magnitude of that achievement.

The play-off game was at Wootton High School on May 4, 2017, and we arrived at a packed gym. Some parents had traveled for Blair, but it was no match for the roaring sidelines of Wootton. Our past struggles and lack of talent would come to haunt us again. We had no middle except for Brenna and Olivia, who would either sub off due to rotations or play outside and right side, leaving the middle open for opposing hits. Having no tall boys for middle meant for that whole rotation we would be vulnerable at the middle position. Despite this, we fought extremely hard, doing our best to try to keep up with Wootton. At times we went on small rallies, only to have Wootton side-out and take the momentum back. There were sparks here and there where we showed much promise. We even took a set off Wootton (which to be honest, none of us expected). However, Wootton, with their taller and more experienced players, handed us a 3-1 defeat.

Although we lost, I knew we were in a good spot. Not only did coed have young talent, but we would not lose many of our players to graduation, which meant we had a good core unit to work with for the future. Shio now had a couple of years of coaching and experience with volleyball under his belt, along with the help of Coach Armstead, who brought in a much-needed emphasis on learning fundamentals and preparing mentally for games.

After our season ended, Coach Chris of the boys varsity team asked if I would join him for practice. Because boys varsity had also made the playoffs—and moved on to the next round—Coach Chris wanted to have his team ready for playoff-level hitting. I was honored and a bit surprised that he asked me, but I knew that any time I could spend with him meant improving my game and more practice, not to mention his humor and company were also something I enjoyed.

I walked into the small gym, and there was Chris, wearing his usual sweatpants and hoodie. He ran hitting drills first and had me hit from outside, then middle, and finally right side. I never kept count, but it had to be somewhere around a couple of hundred sets. With each hit Chris would give me tips on how to change my hitting or how to approach it differently. He also talked about knowing not only how to hit but when to hit.

As a hitter in volleyball, you can get caught up in the thrill of hitting, and like many hitters, I myself also enjoy hitting a lot. I was the type of player who would hit regardless of the set or defense I was playing against, but Chris taught me about different kinds of hits and how to utilize them at particular moments, be it a roll or a tip. I adjusted and mixed in various types of hitting, and I felt my game really start to take on another form.

On the defensive side, Chris had boys run hitting lines while I, along with other players, ran defensive drills. Defense in volleyball is truly an art form and requires not only a heightened sense of discipline but also vigilance. Chris talked about how one can decipher hitting styles and use them to predict where opposing hitters will hit. Just by looking at arm and body positioning, he could tell where hits were going. My mouth dropped wide open! I never knew anything about that, and it completely changed the way I played defense from that moment on. I never thought much about it, but that day, which was supposed to be an ordinary practice session helping out the boys varsity team, ended up helping me in the long run.

The award ceremony for the 2016-2017 season was a little more exciting and comforting to attend. Although we only had a 4-7 record, making the playoffs was a huge deal. I secured another offensive MVP award, along with Joanne, who was awarded defensive MVP, and Jaya was awarded the coaches award.

When I got home from the ceremony, I immediately went upstairs and, like the previous year, locked my award away. Winning trophies never sat well with me, and I spoke to Shio about it many times. It was a formal thing, and all sports did it, but singling out only a few players for awards was not something I liked because volleyball is never about just one person. No matter how good of a hitter, passer, server, blocker, or setter someone is, everyone relies on each other. If you were to break down even a single point, there is so much complexity to it. Someone has to pass a perfect ball to a setter, who then has to make an effort and put that ball in a perfect set for their hitter. The hitter then has to finish the play, and it repeats with many variations. Although we like to pay attention to the point scoring and hitting aspect of volleyball, the true magic lies in everything that leads up to it. It takes a great deal of work to make a single point possible.

There were times during my junior season that stood out to me in particular. The rides back to school after a game were always very intimate times. Given the quiet and peaceful nature of the night rides, I always had time to think about whatever was on my mind. I remember that, during the ride home after our playoff game, I had some time to think to myself and reflect on everything that was happening. The world was full of future possibilities.

As I looked down the aisle and saw my teammates laughing and joking around with each other, I couldn't help but think about the promise I had made to Shio. For some reason I couldn't enjoy that season, or any season for that matter. It's one of the hard things about being an athlete. You try your best to enjoy the good moments, but the bad ones stick with you way more than the good ones. You could win all your games in a season except for just one, and for some odd reason become so fixated on that one loss that you forget about anything good.

Our 2016-2017 season, by all accounts, was a success for Blair, as was told to us by the coaches and head of the athletic department.

We were building something strong, but I wasn't satisfied. I wasn't in the mood for another participation award or another offensive MVP award. I just wanted to love the game I was playing and win.

Chapter 5

My Time with You Changed Me

The offseason before my senior year, I sat down alone and went over everything from the previous two years of my volleyball experience. I had studied and looked over stats and game film—whatever we had, which wasn't much—and really made it my every waking thought to get better at the game. I knew the upcoming season was our last year and final chance at putting coed volleyball on the map so to speak.

I truly feel there exists this level of love for something that is beyond anything I could fully describe in words, a true intrinsic connection or relationship. It's like a type of love and commitment to a sport that courses through every ounce of your body. When you step onto the court, everything becomes secondary, and you are put into this zone of existence where you can leave all your worries behind. I can't really explain it, but there's almost something very spiritual to it. In my first two years, I didn't take the mental aspect of the game that seriously. I often assumed it was like any other sport or any logical thing in life. If you just got stronger and faster, then you could excel at a high level.

Volleyball doesn't work like that. It requires a level of balance between the physical and mental selves. I began to focus more on building the mental aspect of my game. and it was all thanks to someone who made me change my entire approach. Coach Chris, throughout many practices during the 2016-2017 season, would come over and chat with me about various things. We had developed a close bond, even though he was coaching boys varsity. He'd ask me about the team and how we were doing, and I would ask him about game specifics and how to approach various situations during different types of sets or plays. It was really those conversations that changed my whole viewpoint on volleyball and life.

Volleyball is not just a sport. It needs to be a way of life. Your every living and waking moment has to be dedicated to it. During my first two years, I had been solely motivated by extrinsic goals, like winning games or earning trophies, but once my understanding of the sport changed, I began to develop a different kind of respect and reverence for the game. I began to truly love it, and it was the process of volleyball itself that became my driving force. Practices were no longer a burden; they were now something fun to look forward to. I was no longer worried about the outcome of games and, instead, focused on what I could learn from each moment I experienced on and off the court. This change in my approach to volleyball would also find its way into all other aspects of my existence, and I found my whole perspective on life changed as well.

During the summer, I spent hours watching films from various other volleyball games, mostly at the college level. I would watch big programs and try to focus on the details of the game, not so much on the outcomes. Things like rotations and sets.

At Blair I was fortunate to have access to someone who had years of volleyball playing and coaching experience. I studied games coached by Chris by going to as many of his games as I could. He would use lineups in a very particular way, often putting his players in ideal situations where they could fully actualize their talents. His thought processes behind games were very detailed and planned out. He always knew the weaknesses of the team they were playing, and as the game went on, he would make substitutions and tell his players to look for spots or certain tendencies by the other team that they could exploit. He also knew how to utilize his players to their full potential, and most importantly, he coached communication and fundamentals.

As I watched his teams, I could always sense that the group of girls or guys on the floor really meshed together well, and their level of communication with each other, both verbally and nonverbally, was strong. Communication is arguably the single most important thing in volleyball outside fundamentals. A volleyball team can only be as good as their communication.

I tried my hardest to put in hours every day working to master the ins and outs of not only hitting but passing. My hitting was not very good in the sense that I did not have a complete and stable hitting form. I always just jumped randomly and hoped to time it right for a hit, but now I really tried to break down each step and quite literally change my approach. (An approach is what is referred to as a hitter's run-up.) On defense I practiced playing in every position in the back row and especially worked on my footwork. Oftentimes during a game, you could go from watching a ball being set to seeing it fly across the court. You have to react accordingly, which requires great footwork to be able to completely change your body's direction and commit to wherever the ball is going.

I also had the great honor of watching one of the best players in Blair volleyball history: Albert. During my first year on coed, he was a senior on what was an amazing boys varsity team full of pure talent. That first year I was able to soak in the experience of going to all the boys varsity games and watching great players excel at the sport. The best way I can describe Albert is that he had an almost Clark Kent-type persona. When you saw him outside the court in the hallways, you would never think of him as athletic, but on the court he was Superman. He was one of the all-rotation players for Blair that year, and every aspect of his game was excellent, be it serving, passing, blocking, hitting, and even setting.

I took notice of his approach, in particular, and his hitting. Albert could quite literally float in the air for a few seconds and in that short time figure out where to place his hit and then deliver it with ease. Although he did not possess the height of other players in the county, he was often the biggest person on the court and could hit past any defense in front of him. I was able to learn a great deal just by watching players like him but also by what they taught us during practice. We would often go to the varsity boys practices to help out while they were in playoffs, and it was a great time to learn from individual players. Other players were a pool of knowledge about defense and passing. One thing that was very special about that team was their communication. Whether they were ahead or behind in a set, they always prioritized communication on the court. That was something we needed to focus on more in coed.

In our previous two years, I can admit we rarely talked on the court. The one consistent thing Shio always pointed out during each practice and game was how quiet we were. "Communicate, guys. I need to hear you talking to each other!" he would say. I never quite understood the importance of communication until my senior year. Then it all came full circle and made much more sense to me why we were such a poor "team." We were more like a group of talented individuals preoccupied with ourselves rather than a single unit, and it was because of our lack of communication.

Communication in volleyball is twofold. On the one hand, it involves a direct type of communication in the form of talking, but the other lies in body communication. During games, great teams communicate with each other using very specific volleyball language. Words like "side-out," "balls up," "outside," and "tip," among others, are very common, but these deal primarily with verbal communication. An advantage of this type of talk is that you can directly communicate what should be happening on the court to others, but that also means the opposing team can hear what you are saying.

The second type of communication in volleyball—nonverbal communication—is arguably far more important. What you physically do on the court is another way you can communicate with your teammates. Once players on a team play with each other long enough, they start to develop an awareness of each other's playing styles, tendencies, and all aspects of their nonverbal communication. It could be something as simple as how they approach a hit, where they like to be set, or where they will be on the court during a particular play. Once a team can master communication, their chemistry grows, they make fewer errors on the court, and everyone elevates each other's play.

Because I was planning to study psychology, and found it to be a useful tool in any aspect of my life, I also implemented many psychological principles into volleyball. I loved the mental aspect of the game itself. Not solely concepts about handling your emotions or your own frame of mind but, more specifically, how to get into your opponents' heads. I remembered that line from the *Captain America: Civil War* movie when the bad guy, Baron Zemo, talks about how he managed to break up the Avengers, not by going toe to toe with them but by getting them to turn on each other, which made his job easier. That always stuck with me. By intentionally getting into another person's head, not only could you force them to make mistakes, but you could also cause a rift among a team. If the inner foundation of the team is broken, then everything tumbles. You can think of it as very planned-out trash talk.

As I began to study more about the mental aspect of volleyball, I was reminded of our final game of the year during the 2015-2016 season. Not only were we doing poorly in relation to our opponents, but our team also began to collapse upon itself. Players started to get heated, and we began to make more mistakes than usual. I realized a great deal of that was because of the other team getting into our heads whenever they made a play. It could be anything from a little comment here or there or a look that caused more stress, leading to a lack of care for fundamentals on our part. Once a team begins to ignore fundamentals, it spells catastrophe.

The rules of volleyball were also something I looked at for the first time. Coach Chris and Shio had information about those kinds of things, so every now and then I would look for specific rules and also think about referee tendencies, like calls they commonly made or what they looked out for during games. Certain refs, as we all may have experienced, may be known to call certain fouls more than others or look out for certain things more than other refs. Knowing these simple things could gain you an extra advantage over your opponent.

I felt I was beginning to really understand volleyball, but I was only scratching the surface. With each passing day, I found myself discovering more things that greatly aided my abilities to improve.

That entire summer it was hard to get a full night's rest. I was anxiously waiting for the season to start and could not stop thinking about being on the court again. I often thought about our team and how the season would go. All athletes can relate to this. You sometimes become so obsessed with your sport that it begins to take over your life. I walked around with Wilson every day, setting or passing to myself. Any opportunity that arose meant more practice. I was loving volleyball with my every breath. It was one of the best, if not *the* best, summer I'd had in my life up to that point.

As the days inched toward the start of senior year, one day I happened to recall some old memories. I remember closing my eyes, and it was like I was reliving that memory. It was during one of our family volleyball games on our yearly trip to Sandy Point Park several years before. Our family volleyball games had started out as very friendly games, but over the years they had become very competitive. One particular year, things got even more competitive, and bragging rights for the rest of the year were on the line. Everyone, young and old, had gathered, and we split our team based on the prior year's lineup. That particular year there was more trash talk than usual but in a friendly way. The game was very intense. Points were scored back and forth. At times there were arguments about whether a ball was in or out because there were no official court boundaries. It got to the point where it seemed as though every point we scored had to be reviewed by the spectators. No one really knew how to officially play volleyball except for a handful of people. There weren't really any sets, passes, or rotations. The only rule we kept was that there were only three touches allowed on either side. (I can only imagine what it would have been like had we abandoned that rule.) The only objective everyone followed was to do whatever it took to score and stop the other team from scoring. It was neck and neck until the very end, when the other team pulled away to win the game.

As I was reliving that memory, I couldn't stop smiling and beaming with happiness. I had been playing alongside my dad, my uncles, cousins, and people I loved, and then it hit me. How amazing is this sport? Volleyball for me at that moment took on a whole new meaning. It was no longer just a sport for me. It had become a significant part of my life. I had finally hit that sweet spot where I began to not just see a sport but understand the power it can have to give us a way to celebrate life and each other, something we need more of in the world today, if you ask me. This sport which I happened to come across sifting through my attic had changed my life forever.

Chapter 6

I Was Given a Family

As that summer before my senior year came to a close, the real preparations for the season began. Using our old group chat, which I still use to this day—I don't know why we used it, given we had Instagram and Snapchat—we talked a lot about changing the way we had done things over the last two years. In the past we had relied solely on waiting to see who would try out for volleyball and just hoped talent would show up at our court. But the lifeblood of any program is its players. I talked to Shio and Jaya about it in private. We threw around ideas about how we could strengthen our team, and we decided we had to change the way Blair did things. If we wanted to become the *new* Blair coed volleyball, we had to throw away old bad habits and build new ones.

I had secretly talked to a couple of the boys team players throughout the 2016-2017 season. They were classmates I knew and friends I had developed close relationships with. We decided I should talk to them again. Jaya would also talk to some of the girl players, and Shio would do some extra advertising for the sport. We actively sought out new players wherever we could find them.

Tyler and Avery were two boys players who had expressed interest in joining coed. They were on the original 2014-2015 team, which held the best record for Blair coed up to that point in time. They had already won the division for boys varsity and knew that the current team was not as well equipped as their previous teams, so they decided to leave boys and join coed. I remember when I saw Coach Chris for the first time after he found out they were leaving.

He made fun of me for stealing his players. He joked about it and was cool with it, and I'll forever be thankful to him for that.

Jaya had spoken to some players from girls' varsity before the season, and they also expressed interest in joining coed. Two of the girl's team players, Tiffany and Ariel, had played their entire career at Blair. They were excellent and talented volleyball players who would add much-needed depth and strength to the team. Both were powerful servers, amazing passers, and monumental defenders and could even hit when needed. Slowly but surely, we started to build a good team.

The setter position was no issue for us, but Coach Armstead and Shio talked about having multiple setters for the 2017-2018 year. Having a great setter is fine, but having two great setters is fine on steroids. Jaya recruited one of her friends from girls varsity, Fiona. Fi, as was their nickname, had a heart unlike anyone on the team. It didn't matter how far a ball was passed or how bad a pass it was, they would find a way to set it to our hitters. I always joked that if anyone were to be given a green lantern ring for their willpower, it would be them (a comic book reference for all the superhero fans out there). Fiona was also the fire for our team, often being the loudest on the court and never being fazed by outside noise.

Our setting was now set, so to speak, but there was one position we had struggled with the last two years: middle. The middle was the one piece missing from our lineup. We had Brenna, of course, but with how volleyball is played, at some point in the rotation, she would end up subbing out, leaving that part of the court wide open, so we needed other tall players. The middle really sets the tone in volleyball, and having one gives the setter all available options for a set on offense while also perfectly bolstering defense because you have a reliable blockade for one part of the court. No one we knew was available, and school had not started yet, so we decided to hold off on that one for a while.

As I recall this story, it still gives me chills because of how unexpected what came next was. There are those rare moments in life when the universe seems to just hand you an answer, and it's like, "Oh wow, thanks!"

In my senior year of high school, I was assigned Mr. Stelzner for Honors English 12. Mr. Stelzner was a very down-to-earth, wonderful teacher whom seniors the previous year spoke very highly of. He was a massive Star Wars and comic book superhero movie fan, making him someone I could relate to, not to mention the fact that he was one of the greatest teachers at Blair. His classroom was on the first floor, and I can still picture walking into that classroom for the first time. As soon as I stepped through the door, I did what any student does when entering a new classroom: I scanned the layout of the room, noted where the chairs were, and looked for anyone I knew. Since no one I knew was there, I immediately turned to my left and sat near the door. Something about that spot just felt right, almost like the universe was calling me to it. I sat down and waited patiently for other students to arrive. Observing the classroom, I saw posters of various Star Wars films and projects of students from previous years.

All of a sudden, in walked Mr. Stelzner. He was wearing a white button-up shirt with a tie, an outfit he had become famous for wearing at Blair, and was carrying a metal water bottle he had just filled. Music was playing in the background. You could tell by how he walked in that he was in a very upbeat mood. One of my best friends walked in and I yelled in excitement. You know that feeling when you see your best friend in the same classroom as yours? There's no other feeling like it!

Minutes went by and in walked this tall guy I had never seen before. He was wearing glasses, his long black hair was just free-flowing, and he had one of those strap bags at his side that is normally used to carry a laptop. He slowly came in and, a bit awkwardly, I kept my eyes on him from the moment he entered until he sat down to my left, two chairs over. He never realized I was observing him. I could hear my friend talking to me, but his voice seemed to fade away. He shook me, bringing me back to my senses.

"Who is that?"

I asked him.

"That's Noah," my friend said.

And just like that, the universe had handed us our middle on a silver platter. I had finally found what we were looking for. The missing piece of the puzzle quite literally was now in front of me.

I remember sprinting to Coach Shio's classroom with excitement for my bliss tutoring class. Shio looked at me with a confused face as I screamed, "We finally found our middle." He calmed me down and I told him everything. Our only job now was to somehow convince Noah to play volleyball.

Every morning during English, I'd say hello or good morning to Noah, slowly trying to develop a friendship over time. I had to first establish some sort of connection with him, something beyond just being in the same class together. Weirdly enough, during a conversation I was having with my friend about superheroes, Noah joined in, and we started our little discussion trio in class. We talked during class about things like superheroes, movies, and music. I learned that Noah played golf for Blair, so I knew he was athletic, and he obviously had the height we needed.

One fateful day I decided to muster up whatever courage I had and ask him to join coed volleyball. I leaned over, took a deep breath, and finally put it all on the table. "You play any sports in the spring?" I asked. When he shook his head no, my heart slowly upped its beats per minute. "You ever think about joining volleyball? You're tall, so you'd fit right in, and we need a middle desperately right now." I was sure he was going to politely decline. Why would he play a sport he probably never gave a second thought to, but to my surprise, he agreed. I had been sure I would have to try to convince him in some way, maybe talk about the sport or find some way to entice him, but just like that he agreed. Given it was our senior year, he had an open schedule for spring, and he seemed really interested in joining. Had it not been for the fact that I was in class that day, I would probably have yelled so loud that the windows in the room would have shattered.

In my excitement I texted our group chat. Everyone's reaction was similar to mine. I received emojis that I could not decipher, given my lack of knowledge about modern-day texting, but I did understand that the excitement levels were at an all-time high. Slowly, we were building a team that had all the pieces. I remember going home and writing up a lineup. I couldn't stop smiling. I'd draw up plays and rotations we could run, and I could even picture various plays happening right before my eyes. Having a good middle would change our lives forever. Noah may not have realized it at that moment in time, but he wasn't just someone coed desperately needed that year; he was something Blair volleyball as a program had been missing.

The fall semester flew by extremely quickly. I had many chances to go to the girls volleyball home games, where I met up with old friends and chatted with Coach Chris. It was also an opportunity to recruit players to coed. Shio dropped by sometimes, and we scouted players that coed needed.

That year, girls' volleyball held a fundraising game where students played against staff to raise money as well as collect food items to donate to various food drives. I grabbed a couple of friends, and we dropped by my home to pick up anything we could to donate. My parents were confused when they saw my friends and me grabbing cans of food from our pantry, but once I told them why I was doing it, they gladly offered more food to give. We arrived at school and walked to the main gym. It was a strange scene that attracted the eyes of anyone we passed. A group of high school students carrying loads of canned goods and barely holding it all together.

Girls' varsity and junior varsity had already been prepping inside, along with various staff members. I must be honest in that I gave the staff no shot at winning the game, given how volleyball worked. On the girls side, you essentially had a team who had played together for months and some even longer than that and, on the staff side, a group of randomly selected individuals had to somehow come together who had to not only figure out how to communicate but play volleyball together.

To my surprise, not only did the staff communicate well, they outplayed the girls! My jaw dropped to the ground as I witnessed many staff members execute perfect plays, be they digs, serves, receives, or hits. It got close toward the end. In one play the staff served it over to the girls, who then received it, set and hit it back over. Not only did the staff defense dig up the hit, they somehow set their outside. I remember that play vividly. The outside hitter struck with all his might right in the middle of all six players. Everyone in the gym went crazy. The staff ended up winning that game by a couple of points, and like everyone in the gym, I was lost for words. I walked down to the court and approached all the players I knew, poking fun at them for how they played. Of course, they responded with excuses that it was just a game for fun and they hadn't really been trying, but I teased them about that day for a long time afterward.

Volleyball season was fast approaching, and to signal the beginning of our new journey, we created a new group chat, as was the tradition every year. That was always something really hard to do. Over the course of a season, you would have such amazing moments with your teammates and share such great memories. But now that season was officially coming to a close, and a new chapter was beginning.

On Monday, November 27, 2017 at 12:42 p.m., Jaya sent a text that officially began our season: "Hey, guys, if you're playing coed we are having an interest meeting tomorrow in room 333 at 3:30!"

Chapter 7

Moments That Made Me Happy

Excited as ever about the fast-approaching volleyball season, everyone pitched ideas about upcoming events we could host and potential drills we could design for practices. Winter sports were still in progress, but we wanted to have a major head start on our season. We quickly acclimated the newcomers to the team, having everyone meet and greet each other and going over important things to know about the sport and the kinds of things to expect.

After Jaya sent that text regarding the interest meeting, I remember sitting and thinking long and hard about the number 333. I was sure it wasn't 333. I kept wondering what was in room 333, but thankfully, someone corrected Jaya, informing her that it was room 233, Coach Shiotani's room.

Jaya had planned workouts with the girls for the upcoming weeks as a way for people to get into shape before the season started. The earlier we started to work on our physical fitness, the more time we would have to focus on volleyball-related things during the early weeks of the season. Fiona mentioned a gym they and their parents were renting at Woodside Urban Park in downtown Silver Spring that had a volleyball net available." They asked about having a sort of trial run practice before the season to get some game time and, more importantly, get the new players situated and the team to start bonding.

The summer and fall seasons had been so quiet, and now, all of a sudden, things were kicking up again. It was exciting. In typical coed volleyball fashion, we could not decide on a date for the practice session. We went back and forth, which took forever, but thankfully, modern technology would be our saving grace with the advent of polling systems that saved us much-needed time. In previous seasons we did not have the luxury of a preseason-type practice, but the opportunity to get some volleyball-playing time was worth the hassle it took to set it up.

Some people couldn't make it, but the turnout was good enough. Noah, Tyler, Jaya, Fiona, Brenna, Olivia, and I showed up. A friend of Noah's also tagged along. He was a tennis player and also as tall as Noah. We arrived and greeted each other with smiles and an outpouring of excitement. Just the view of a volleyball and net melted our hearts. As always we started that practice with peppering to warm up. (Peppering is a volleyball term for when two players exchange passes with each other to get their arms loose and to warm up before any type of intense drills.)

Something about that practice felt different than anything I had felt during my first two years with coed. There was a certain feel in the air, an understanding of the possibility that we had something special brewing, given the kind of talent and skill level we had that year. We finished our peppering, and Jaya concluded with a scream. "Hitting lines!" she yelled.

We all took a ball and lined up on both sides of the net. Having two setters gave us the freedom to run multiple hitting lines and work more with the new players, which was something new and much needed. Noah was near the net, working on his hitting approach, learning the basics of volleyball, and getting an introduction to his role as a middle. The returning players from the 2016-2017 season picked up right where we had left off. Our hitting was strong and consistent. Olivia, with her towering height, found it easy to hit strong and accurate balls to various points of the court. Brenna was working alongside Noah, given her experience and extensive knowledge about playing in the front middle position. Tyler was receiving and digging up hits to work on his defense. It was truly a spectacular thing to witness.

Sometimes, I got lost just observing everyone else. I couldn't help but smile at the team we were building. Things were starting to change: Blair was finally arriving and volleyball was finding its place among the successful programs at school.

We worked on hitting lines for quite a bit. Jaya then signaled to switch over to passing drills. Although it seems easy in volleyball, passing is often the most difficult thing to do. In practice there isn't a great deal of pressure, so your body is much more relaxed, but during games, emotions are at an all-time high, which can interrupt fundamentals. Passes that you could normally make in your sleep may end up being shanked. (When a ball is shanked, it is received poorly, which makes it unplayable or difficult for other players to get to.)

We started with very simple passes. Jaya or Fiona would throw the ball underhand while we stood some feet away. Although it was a simple drill, we knew that to get where we wanted, we had to start at the absolute basics and really work on perfecting our craft. Even for the kinds of skills and abilities we were strong in, focusing on the fundamentals helped us create a strong foundation to build on.

At first the newcomers like Noah struggled with passing. He wasn't used to body positions required in volleyball, and I could see the confusion on his face, but with time he improved greatly. The experienced players passed with ease. We then quickly transitioned to more intense passing. Slowly but surely, we made our way through increasingly difficult drills. Serving was next.

Serving was something I loved extremely. Serving can be one of the most overlooked things in volleyball because, on the surface, its primary role is to begin a set point, but it carries a great deal of importance. Serving can be the difference between earning a free point or giving one away. Over time, serving errors add up and greatly impact the final scoresheet. I had been working on jump serving all summer and attempted a few. Let's just say they looked like airplanes taking off on a runway when, instead, they should have been going downward. I watched as each player served in their own unique way. There were jump serves, floats, top spins, basic serves, and everything in between.

We ended our practice with a mini scrimmage game to get some game time in before tryouts. In one particular play, Olivia served one of her float serves, which looked like a moving target coming at you. Tyler received it effortlessly and sent a perfect pass to Jaya. Jaya set Noah a perfect ball, and it was like watching everything unfold in slow motion. Fiona and I waited for his hit, expecting a net shot or for the ball to be hit out, but what came next all happened so quickly. As Noah's hand made contact with the ball, in a matter of seconds, it flew between us like a meteor heading toward the floor. It struck the floor with a loud bang that echoed in the gym. Everyone stopped for a moment. We were frozen in our shoes. Noah himself did not seem bothered, as if that kind of hit was usual for him. At that moment it hit us just how good this team could be if we got things right.

We ended on a good note and packed our things.

Over the next couple of days, Jaya organized some more workouts with the girls. We went back and forth about preparations and what to work on. Getting in shape before tryouts was a priority for us because it would give us a head start with practice, as opposed to previous years when we had to spend the first couple of weeks readjusting our bodies to volleyball.

On Wednesday, January 31st, there was an interest meeting in Coach Shiotani's room. This was a month before the season, but he wanted to get a headcount for how many people were coming and then get the word out about coed volleyball. Everyone showed up. Shio handed us some paperwork and gave us instructions about mandatory forms. We introduced ourselves to each other and some new people joined.

On Tuesday, February 27, 2018, at 11:59 p.m. on the dot, we all received a text from Ariel, one of the girls' varsity players who was planning to join coed that year. The text read: "Also I just got cleared but I'm not allowed to play volleyball for probably a long while (as in months), so I can't play coed."

Like everyone, I was disheartened. I thought to myself, *Please don't let this be true*. I was hoping to wake up from a dream or wishing that she was playing some sort of prank on us.

Ariel was one of the best players Blair volleyball had ever seen. Her skills as an all-around player were second to none. Her loss was significant.

I was a little comforted when Noah, in his truest, classic Noah self, replied to Ariel: "**Just play anyway.**"

I laughed a little. Although we lost a crucial piece of the team, I still had hope because of how much depth we had that year, not to mention Noah's fun personality to keep us grounded.

Chapter 8

Crouched and Ready, I Wait Desperately

We practiced for a month leading into the season. Given limitations and such, we mostly stuck to gym workouts or at-home volleyball practice, sneaking in whatever playing time we could as a team. There were rules about coaches and joint practices outside the season, which I never really understood, but we did whatever we could and whatever was allowed. Players who were confirmed to tryout spread the word about volleyball during class, and whatever position they held in school now became a platform for them to spread information about the upcoming volleyball season. I had friends who were working with BNC (Blair Network Communications), so they were able to make an announcement about tryouts during the morning InfoFlow session that aired every day at school.

Tryouts were to be held in the main gym, starting March 1st, from 3:30 to 5:30 p.m. On the days leading up to the first tryout, everything was normal. Then, late one night when I was in my room, working on some assignments, my phone suddenly rang. I could see it was my dad calling, and it was unusual that he would call that late at night. He was supposed to be home a couple of hours earlier, but I just assumed something at work held him back. I picked up the phone but couldn't hear anything. Then I heard his voice in the background but couldn't make out any words. The call only lasted seconds and then ended.

I know my dad really well. It was weird that he would end the call in a matter of seconds without saying anything. He'd usually say, "Bye," or "Never mind," so something felt off. As I sat there thinking, I felt anxiety slowly overtake me. I thought I was overthinking it and that it was probably nothing, but just as my mind relaxed a bit, my mom came sprinting into the room with a worried look on her face. At that moment I knew something had happened.

As a child you have a certain connection with your parents. It's kind of hard to describe, but it's almost like you can sense when things are off even though you may not be in their presence. I prayed I was wrong and that it was not a big deal, but hearing the words from my mom that night almost shattered me. She said Dad had been in an accident coming home from work and that he needed to be picked up. Without even thinking, we hopped into a car and raced to him.

The human mind will always deep dive into all sorts of scenarios. You tend to forget anything else happening in your life, and all you can really think about is that one other person who needs you at that moment.

We arrived at the scene and saw the wreckage. Thankfully, no one was seriously injured, but my dad had some trouble walking properly, and to be safe we took him to the hospital that night. To lighten the mood, I went up to him and whispered, "And you call yourself a professional driver." We both laughed, and seeing his smile eased my worries a little.

On our way to the hospital, I asked him what had happened. He said something about how he was thinking about me while driving, and then it all just happened in a split second. I was confused a little. "Why were you thinking about me?" I asked.

Before he could answer, we arrived at the hospital. It took a while to see a doctor, which gave me some time to think. We'd had a normal father-son disagreement a few days before. I sat there in the waiting room and looked around. It was one of those moments that made me reflect on my current situation. I remember observing whatever was in front of me. I saw parents with their children, some young people in front of me, people of all different types and backgrounds. It really brings you back down to earth when you see those kinds of things. We tend to take our little blessings in life for granted, but the universe tends to remind us about them in really strange ways.

As we were waiting, my dad told me to go home because he knew I had school the next day. "You should go home and rest up for tomorrow," he said.

I paused for a bit. Here he was, in the hospital right after an accident that could have easily gone sideways and taken his life, yet he had my well-being on his mind. I didn't understand the moment at the time, but it later hit me what kind of man he was that night.

Parents of all types never want to see their children in any sort of pain. They always put us kids first, and we sometimes may not show that same love back to them, but at that moment I knew this guy was special. Funny enough, it would also be the reason our argument days prior instantly evaporated.

Volleyball seemed to be nonexistent for me the next day. All I could think about was my dad. I texted Shio about it, and he gave me some words of support, told me missing tryouts wouldn't be a big deal, and that I should take whatever time I needed. Volleyball had always been a safe haven for me, so I decided to get right back into it.

As I laid in bed at home, I opened up my phone to look at the messages that had been blowing up on my notifications board.

Although I wasn't physically with my team, those messages were a way of staying connected with everyone. The players were all talking about various things. The big gym was finally ours now that winter sports were over. Ariel was going to drop by to watch the team even though she couldn't play. When I popped in to chat and let everyone know I wouldn't be coming that day, Jay responded: **Hope everythings okay @Aziz Baig**

I was lucky enough to have these amazing people in my life, and I couldn't stop smiling at all of it. I had some time to think, so like any normal person, I sort of went through a little timeline of my own life, and it really started to hit me how cool life was. We can become so preoccupied with everything happening in our lives that we sometimes forget the real treasures are the people in our lives. They are there for us in times of sadness, they make us laugh, and they give meaning to our existence.

I walked into school that day pretty scared. I wasn't with my dad, and I just wanted him to be safe. As I walked into the main gym, my eyes lit up. There were like a hundred people there. I first thought maybe they were there for something else, but to my surprise they were all trying out for coed. I must admit I cried a little. I know for most it wasn't something to cry about, but for me it was. Shio, Brenna, and I had started this program together, and we wanted to build it into something special. To see the turnout difference from our first year to now was truly something spectacular. Coed volleyball was slowly becoming a serious sport and gaining momentum.

Tryouts were wonderful. Players of all skill levels came. Drills went smoothly, and the newcomers were all very talented, given their previous experience with the sport. Cuts were hard to make. It was sad seeing the group shrink by the day. On the third day we were down to final cuts. For the most part I knew who was going to be on the team. Brenna and I were in our third year, along with Shio. We were sort of the holy trinity of coed volleyball. Jaya was our setter, returning from last year. Noah made it as our only tall middle other than Brenna. Tiffany from girls' volleyball made it. Olivia returned from last year. My cousin, Muhammad, also returned after much enticing on my part. Avery and Tyler from the boy's team made it. Elisabeth also returned. And we had some new players. Fiona was another setter from girls. River was a new player, along with Edward, Mizan, Abby, Sarah, Ruben, Miles, and Isabelle. We had a mix of young and experienced players. It was important to build a team that could compete now but also create a foundation for the future. That was it. That was our team.

After final cuts were made, we huddled around coaches Shiotani and Armstead. They congratulated us on making the team and promised us it was going to be a special season.

As always, captains needed to be chosen before the start of practice, so we held a vote. Jaya was the clear-cut first choice for head captain. She was both the setter and an experienced player on the team, and her charisma and personality fit well as a strong leader who could empower her teammates. Shio and Armstead wanted just a co-captain this year, deciding to stay away from a three-captain strategy, given our more intimate team this year. Because we knew each other and were friends, there was no need for a third captain. Tiffany's name was mentioned, but Tiff shied away from it. Tyler and Avery didn't care much about it, so they said no. Brenna was a perfect choice, given her tenure at Blair and her close friendship with Jaya, not to mention her leadership outside of volleyball. But for some reason, Shio again chose me.

I wanted Brenna to be co-captain because she had also started this journey along with Shio and me, but Shio pulled me aside and had a little chat with me about it. We both had talked early on in our time together about volleyball and the future. I had made him a promise which I vowed would come true at some point.

Captains were set and the season was officially in progress.

Chapter 9

My Heart Fully Committed to You

One day during my first year with coed, before the season started, I'd had a chat with Coach Shio in his room. I remember walking into room 233, and there he was, wearing his flannel shirt and eating the candy he always hid in his desk. We didn't know each other too well, but we slowly started to develop a close bond with each other. It was our first year in the sport officially, and we each went through much growing together.

That day I pulled up a nearby chair and sat directly across from him. I thanked him for everything up to that point and we discussed things like roster plans and the upcoming season. I really got a sense about who he was in that talk of ours, and it remains the most important conversation we've had in our time together with volleyball.

During our conversation, we brought up the history of coed volleyball and where it was at that point in time among the other sports programs at Blair. I told him about my thoughts on the sport and why I joined. Of course, I loved the sport to death, but on top of that, I wanted to change the culture of coed volleyball at Blair. We both were on the same page when it came to that.

At the time he was a little doubtful about whether or not we could change the culture in such a short time, let alone become a winning program, but I told him something that day that we had never forgotten since. I looked him directly in the eye and said,

"Shio, I promise you that we will win the division by the time I am done with coed volleyball." It was a bold statement, and I immediately regretted saying it. But I had felt this strange force take me over and I was overwhelmed with confidence. We both knew that winning a division title wasn't something that could happen overnight. It would take a long time, years maybe, for us to not only turn volleyball around but make coed into a program that could win consistently. I walked out of his room that day and coed volleyball was forever changed, only I didn't know it then.

I often think about that promise I made to Shio. It was no longer just an option to work toward being the best; it had become a requirement. Whatever hopes we had or whatever thoughts we had about this sport were no more. From now on, win or lose, we were going to give it our all and work toward a new standard of Blair volleyball.

Chapter 10

I'm So Happy
When I'm On the Court

During the first couple of weeks of the 2017-2018 season, everything ran smoothly. The practices were crucial for us in those beginning weeks because it was the first time we as a collective group were all playing together. Talent can only take you so far; it takes time for players to mesh together, especially in volleyball. Building an unconscious awareness of each other on the court and having an established communication link takes time and practice. The setter and hitter relationship is one thing that has to be established early on. Like the previous season, Jaya and I were going back and forth about the Marvel vs DC comics superhero debate. We were both avid comic book movie watchers and were just coming off seeing *Black Panther*, which had been released in February.

Having a strong relationship with your setter is important, not only for the aspect of the sport itself but also for the teammate aspect. We were both captains and needed to make sure we had each other's back and maintained a constant level of open communication. It was important that we create relationships beyond volleyball, whether that meant sharing each other's hobbies or talking about personal interests. It's the little details you learn about each other that solidify a true relationship and build strong teams in sports.

Noah, along with the other newcomers, was getting more and more situated and comfortable with the game. His approaches were improving greatly, and his feel for hitting, as well as his understanding of responsibilities in the middle position, were getting better with each play. The underclassmen were added to the group and introduced to the dreadful duties of being a new player. Blair had a tradition of having the underclassmen learn how to pull the floor— essentially cleaning it before games to ensure the court had no dirt. Blair's volleyball court (also the basketball court) was notorious for being slippery. That could make games really difficult given how much movement is required on the floor, and slips could lead to serious injuries.

The starting six were beginning to click, but our practices were not helping us as much as we needed or wanted. We were limited in our ability to mimic the atmosphere during games as well as real scenarios we might encounter when we actually played other teams. Shio decided for the first time ever that Blair would schedule a preseason match.

High School sports generally don't have preseason games, but coaches can talk and discuss having a sort of practice game for their players to get some idea of what games are like and to get their bodies in shape, as well as their minds in the correct mentality for the season. John F. Kennedy High School—or Kennedy, as we called it—graciously agreed to hold a preseason match at their home court. (Thank you, Kennedy!) Shio scheduled the game for March 14, 2018, after school.

While all this was going on, it was a scary moment in time for everyone. Headlines all over the news were flooded with information and talk about the recent shootings that had taken place in Florida at Marjory Stoneman Douglas High School. It was a very terrifying time for all of us, especially high school students. Just coming to school felt worrisome because the thought that lingered in everyone's minds was what if such a thing were to happen at Blair.

Blair, along with all other high schools in Montgomery County, instituted new policies and guidelines for students, staff, and after-school programs. Security was more prevalent and on high alert. It felt strange coming to school after that event transpired. No longer did it feel safe to be outside the walls of Blair. I must admit at times I felt afraid and lost. I couldn't imagine what those kids in Florida were going through that day, witnessing what happened. They came to school as if it was a regular day, only to have their whole world flipped upside down, to see their friends gone in an instant. I would often question why those things happened. Why couldn't all the bad things just stop for once?

Yet through it all, something gave not only me but everyone hope. After the events at Stoneman Douglas, millions of people around the world, people who were mostly my age, came together and stood up for all the injustices that were happening. It was amazing to see such courage, such hope, brought about by people society considered adolescent and immature.

For the most part, we had left that topic out of our practices and inner circles of volleyball, but after a walkout was announced in response to the recent events, Ms. Boule, our athletic director, sent out an email to athletes about participating in it. We had to face our fears and tackle the topic head-on together. There was no more hiding the issue.

Coach Shiotani forwarded me a reminder sent to him by Ms. Boule. I texted everyone: "Hey. Just FYI, Ms. Boule just sent a reminder to us saying that the walkout Wednesday counts as an unexcused absence, which means you are not allowed to participate in the scrimmage (poor planning on my part) – Shiotani."

Brenna Levitan, who played for coed, was one of the students in charge of the walkout. She is without a doubt one of the most brave and inspiring individuals I have ever met in my life. She seized the opportunity and stood up for what she believed in. We knew she had been closely involved with many of the events at school and in the country about protests and such, but we weren't aware of how involved she really was. At the time few people knew about her involvement in the walkout. Jaya decided to hold a meeting during practice to figure things out and have a dialogue about everything that had been going on.

On March 12, 2018, two days before our scrimmage game against Kennedy High School, we held our meeting after practice. Everyone gathered around coaches Armstead and Shiotani. I looked around and saw everyone's exhausted postures. Some were on the floor, others with their hands to their sides as they gasped for air. Shio repeated Ms. Boule's announcement and asked for a show of hands about who was staying or leaving. For the most part, everyone was staying.

As Shio's eyes scanned our group in a panoramic fashion, his eyes locked on Brenna as she raised her hand. Brenna announced that she was one of the individuals responsible for the walkout and that she wouldn't make it to our scrimmage. Shio gave her his full support. along with all of us. Volleyball was our team priority, but at that moment amidst all the chaos in the country, we were behind Brenna 100 percent. Whatever she needed to do, we would fully support her.

We closed our meeting and practice by putting our arms together and yelling, "Blair, on three. One . . . two . . . three . . . Blair!" Unbeknownst to all of us, we were a family, and no matter what was happening around us in our collective or individual lives, we could always find comfort in each other and this sport of ours.

As I was sitting in my room a few days later, my cousin yelled, calling me downstairs to our living room. I thought something bad had happened, but he immediately directed my attention to the TV as he was pointed at a particular person. I couldn't make out who it was at first with the crowd, but then I saw a glimpse of blonde hair floating among a sea of people. I knew who it was. It was Brenna! I ran to the TV. "Oh my god, it's Brenna." My father and uncle both looked at me confused. I immediately texted the group chat.

We cheered and felt so proud of her. It was so awesome to know that someone so inspiring and uplifting was literally a teammate we saw on a daily basis and now she was on TV, inspiring millions of people, including us! It gave us all a sort of confidence boost. No matter what happened that year, we knew our duties as students and people would forever mean something more to the greater good of everyone around us. Hearing and seeing Brenna was emotional, to say the least. When she spoke, we all felt her honesty. When we looked into her eyes, we could see how inspired and hopeful she was and how determined she was to stand up for what was right. She is a truly remarkable and wonderful person!

I never thought much about it, but as I often look back at that particular moment in time during my senior year, I have come to appreciate another dimension volleyball brought into my life. Not so much the sport itself but our relationship as a group, or any group for that matter. During a time so dark and so unknown, it is important to have someone—or a group of people—there for you that you can not only feel comfortable with but who you can also comfort. Volleyball gave us a safe space to be with each other. It became a safe haven of sorts. If anyone ever needed anything, we were there to wrap our arms around them. Volleyball would end up becoming our emotional lifeline. It would teach us that even through the darkest of times, we all need to be together, and when, at times, it felt like there was no hope, we knew we could always find it as long as we knew where to look. Through love and togetherness, we could overcome whatever it was that happened to us.

On the day of the game, we all texted each other about rides and who was taking who to Kennedy. Noah was my ride, along with my cousin Muhammad. We met up in the cafeteria and headed out. Along the way Noah handed me his auxiliary power cord and asked me to play a song to get us all hyped before the game. I didn't really have any type of loud or hype music in my playlist, but I had heard about a new song that had been released that year called "God's Plan" by Drake. I was aware of Drake's lyrical talents and musical genius, so I decided to put it on. We all moved to the beat, and something about his lyrics captivated us. That song was special for the season, and at that moment it became the staple pregame song we listened to during our warmups.

Jaya arrived at Kennedy before anyone else did. She was scouting their team as they warmed up. She texted the group: "I'm at Kennedy. They serve well but they don't serve receive super well."

I asked about their hitting to which she responded:

> "2 deep rolls but haven't seen anything else yet. They seem to only be able to do stuff off really good sets. Can't tip or free ball super well."

She and I had discussed changing up our pregame routines before the season started. Normally, Coach Armstead did not like us watching other teams because she felt we might end up focusing too much on them and not enough on us, but that year we needed to scout teams if we wanted to learn about their tendencies.

Jaya added that they had tall people and could rally, but I wasn't too worried. Especially after Noah assured me, with a smile on his face, that it wasn't going to be a problem.

We arrived at Kennedy and pulled into their parking lot. As we entered through the front doors, our bright red colors, a stark contrast to the radiant green of Kennedy, drew a great deal of attention from students in the hallways. We could feel the tension slowly building as we made our way to their gym. Among some of the players missing that day were Brenna, Olivia, because of a knee injury, and Miles, who had recently joined the team.

Kennedy's gym was smaller in height compared to Blair's. Our high ceiling gave us more leeway with how we passed and our abilities to save certain passes. Kennedy's low ceiling meant we had to be careful with how we passed or approached our game.

If there is one element that teams can't account for in high school volleyball, it is the ceiling heights. As a team you grow accustomed to a particular height, and because each school has a different ceiling height, it can either hinder or bolster your performance on the court. It was also extremely hot in the Kennedy gym, which can also affect how you play because humidity can influence ball movement, not to mention speed up the usual rate of player exhaustion.

Their small gym was filled with students who came to watch.

Although it wasn't a game that carried any real weight, it mattered greatly to us.

Shio announced the starting lineup and we were off.

We started the game poorly. Kennedy served over and started with an early lead. Our passes were good but not on target to the setter. Fiona had to run back and forth to reach our passes and could not get their feet set to give a good set to hitters. We rallied some points back and Shio called timeout. We were not clicking as a team. Hitting was godawful. Most of my hits were either hitting the net or going out. Noah had a hard time with transitions and defense. Tyler, Avery, and Tiffany were all struggling with the back row. Our inexperience and lack of playing time together really showed. Somehow, someway, we clawed our way back and won the first set.

During the pregame huddle for the second set, Coach Armstead came over and gave us a rundown of our errors during the first set. We made it a mini goal to focus more on things we could do as a team and gave each other support as we broke the huddle. I looked at everyone on the court and told them not to worry. I hadn't been doing much as a captain, and I needed to start changing my approach. I began yelling and getting louder with each play. If we scored, I ran over and high-fived whoever made a play. If we made a mistake, I told everyone to forget about it and move on to the next play. Slowly, our bond grew, but not too much. We rallied some points and Kennedy nearly came back to tie it, but we pulled through with their serving errors and our last-minute kills to go up 2-0.

The third and final set is probably the scariest one in volleyball. That is when anything could go wrong and momentum could swing in an instant. Because Kennedy was the home team, all they needed was a little energy to carry them through an entire set and, possibly, the rest of the game. It is common to find headlines in the world of volleyball where a team rallied from a 2-0 deficit to come back and win 3-2. I did not want that to be us that day. We were tired and barely holding together. As I looked over, I saw my teammates on the sidelines cheering us on. It gave me some energy to feed off of, and I began yelling at my teammates, getting them excited. If they made a play, I made sure to celebrate with them in whatever childish manner I knew.

Before the start of the third set, as the referee checked our lineup and rotation, I had a moment of realization. I went over to everyone and instructed them not to play at 100 percent. They all looked at me a little confused. Because Kennedy would end up seeing us in the regular season, I did not want them to know every one of our plays, strengths, or weaknesses. I instructed hitters not to strike too hard and for passers not to do anything fancy like dive or sprint across the court. It sounded like a terrible idea, but I knew how hard it can be in volleyball to play a team multiple times and win all of them. I even kept all this from Shio because I knew it would upset him.

At the beginning of the third set, Kennedy and Blair traded strong serves. Kennedy had the momentum then it swung to us and then back to them. We were going back and forth when, finally, we were able to close the deal and sweep Kennedy 3-0. That was a hard-fought win, and although it was ugly, we had plenty of things to celebrate. But more importantly, we had many mistakes to work on. We traded handshakes with Kennedy and huddled in our little corner behind the sidelines.

Shio started by congratulating us but then the bad news struck. We knew we had played badly, but hearing stats individually only drove the dagger deeper. So many of our points were due to

Kennedy's mistakes. It was tough to sit through all that, but it was necessary for us to hear if we wanted to get better. I pulled Shio aside, away from everyone, and told him everything about my mindset during the third set. "Oh, by the way, I told everyone to play bad on purpose during the last set," I whispered.

"What!" he responded. He looked as if someone had informed him candy had been stolen from his desk.

"I didn't want them to see us at our best. If they see us play well then they can learn everything about us and use it against us the next time they play us in the regular season," I explained.

Shio nodded in agreement, although he still was a little upset about how we went about it. Normally, Shio would be against such an idea and likely never allow us to do something like that, but luckily, we won the game, so it all worked out in the end.

We packed our things and left. Although the game meant nothing as far as the regular season was concerned, it was a great thing for us to reflect on as we moved forward, not to mention the fact that winning any game carries with it a great feeling and morale boost. We had a lot to work on and, at the same time, some confidence moving forward.

Chapter 11

The Feeling I Get is Always New

I can remember the days leading up to my first ever volleyball game at Blair during my first year with coed. It was on March 21, 2016, and a night game on top of that at 7:15, however, it was an away game. Our practices had been so fun that I sometimes forgot I was on an actual team. Because most of our team was inexperienced, we had extreme levels of pregame jitters. It being an away game made it that much more nerve wracking. As soon as I stepped off the bus, my heart immediately started beating louder and faster. I could feel every pump of blood, and it only intensified with each passing second. The underclassmen and new players all had the same feeling inside.

As we began warming up, the opposing players walked in. As fate would have it, Sherwood was our season opener. Players who were already at Blair and had played previously for the school knew how good Sherwood was. They had, more times than not, won their division and were always in playoff contention.

Christine, our senior setter, had given us the rundown of coed volleyball throughout the week leading up to our first game. Like any sport, certain programs are either up or down, and then you have your consistent winners. Shio was also new to the sport, so he was learning things along the way as well. I can tell you that he wasn't too excited that his first official game as a head coach was against one of the best teams in the county.

As Sherwood walked in, a sea of blue took over half the bleachers. Parents, along with friends and the boys varsity team, watched as we went through our warmups. The way it worked in high school volleyball was that there was a clock in the gym, counting down from 30 minutes. Around the 16th or 17th minute, both teams would have a joint practice on the floor, each on their side of the net, doing their own unique warmups for about five minutes. Captains were called during this time, along with head coaches, to speak with the referee about rules, court specifications, and the coin toss. Both teams would then each have the whole court to themselves for about six or seven minutes.

When the captains were called to the end of the net near the officiating table, I remember feeling like I was in the wrong place. It was weird being there for the first time. It was my first year, yet there I was, doing the coin toss. Christine was much more relaxed than I was. Away teams would always pick for the coin toss. For us it didn't seem to matter whether we won the toss, we just needed to survive what was coming. As the referee talked to us, I remember looking over at Sherwood's captains. They were relaxed and calm, a stark contrast to my own nervous nature and the pounding fear in my heart. They won the coin toss, we shook hands, and back to warmups we went.

Teams would continue to practice until the sound of a buzzer signaled the end of warmups. The coaches would then proceed to have their starting six players occupy their end line to shake hands with the other team.

That first game was also my first time learning about the ins and outs of volleyball, including rituals. Each team has its own way of prepping for a game, and music is a big part of it. Home teams controlled which songs were played, not only during their warmups but for the opposing teams as well. At Blair we usually played a hype song during our time and a boring song for the opposing team.

Warmups were also very ritualistic. We usually started with basic passing drills rather than hitting lines. Passers and defenders worked on blocking and hit receives while hitting lines were going on. Serving was the cherry on top right before game time. Because we were the away team, we went first. The Sherwood players watched with their eagle eyes, noting every move we made. It made our drills that much harder. I must admit, we were not very good. Our passing was way off target, our serves were inconsistent, often hitting the net or flying way out of bounds. Hitting was just target practice for the net.

The buzzer sound came again. It was really loud and often unexpected. Our turn was over. Sherwood was next.

You always hear that saying, "Don't judge a book by its cover." I hoped that was true as I watched Sherwood practice. It was like watching a professional team. The level of skill they showed compared to us was night and day. Their passes seemed effortless, their hitting was rock solid and fast, and their serving was a work of art. They could even jump serve! I was terrified as I watched. I knew there was no way we were going to win.

I thought hard about all I had learned in prior practices. Shio and Christine did their best to teach us the fundamentals and county rules each day. On the surface, volleyball can seem both easy and hard. The easy part lies in the fact that you just hit a ball. The hard part lies in the fact that it's not just about hitting a ball.

There are six people on either side of the court, separated by the net. The net serves as both the divider between the two teams and a reference point. The line under the net cannot be crossed. The court is outlined by a rectangular box that signals where the ball must hit inside. The six-man team is built with three boys and three girls, one setter, and the option of a libero. (A libero, who is generally the best passer on a team, is a defensive player who can only play in the back row.) The setter can either be a boy or a girl, depending on the team's preference. Each player occupies a space on the court. These spaces are used to refer not only to positions but help with rotations. (Rotations are when, after an earned point, a team must spin, moving on to the next position.) With each rotation, everything changes. You have to be conscious about where you are in conjunction with another player and be sure not to cross any other players (depending on county rules). A girl must touch the ball at least once before it is hit over the net, with the exception of a serve or a direct pass-over on serve receive. Players may not touch the net nor hit the net's two endpoints, also called antennas. It was a lot to take in, but over time we learned each rule slowly and brought it all together. The trick was to get to a point where everyone knew where they needed to be in order to make our games more comfortable and smoother.

Shio wrote his lineup and called us over for a huddle before the match. He told us to stay relaxed and just do our best. To me it sounded like he was telling us, "Guys, we're losing for sure, but good luck." He had a way about him that really made us all stay calm even in the tensest situations. Usually, he'd crack a joke or do something funny to ease the tension a bit.

Prior to getting situated in our rotations, I had a quick chat with our setter, Christine, about the basics of volleyball again. In a split second, due to my worries, I seemed to have forgotten everything

I had learned. I needed a light refresher. By light, I mean a whole recap from beginning to end, of course. Christine quickly rushed over the basics, and we lined up in our positions. I was so lost that I had to ask Christine and Joanne, our libero, about where I was supposed to be all the time. It was embarrassing.

Then, seemingly out of nowhere, I heard the sound of a whistle, which meant the game had now officially started.

Sherwood served over, and I remember seeing the ball in slow motion as Joanne passed the ball to Christine. I was quiet the entire time, even though I should have been yelling to make it look like I knew what I was doing. Christine set to the outside player, our other senior captain, who was a first-year player like me. He swung straight into the net. Sherwood jumped and cheered. Their side of the bleachers was alive. Our side was quiet.

Sherwood served again. This time the ball came to me. It was like watching a bullet coming at me. I put my arms together and attempted to give a good pass to Christine. The ball flew across from her, and luckily, she was able to get it. She set the ball, and again we had another hitting error.

Sherwood continued to control the game. With our mistakes they didn't have to try much. We never communicated and there was no life in our team. They easily ran us off on their home court, three sets to none. If there was ever a list of mistakes a team could make in volleyball, we made all of them. After the game I remember feeling completely broken at how the game turned out and, more importantly, how I played.

Like always, Shio was there to offer guidance and a silver lining. I wish I could recall his words exactly, but he said something along the lines of not allowing that game to define us as a team moving forward, and he encouraged us to think of it like an experience we could always refer back to and draw lessons from. There are times during a season in any sport that is crucial for how a team will evolve and grow. We were lucky to have someone like Shio who could bring out hope and smiles even when we could only see despair.

Chapter 12

Like the Opening of a Story, So Very Short

Our season opener for the 2017-2018 season was scheduled as an away game at Walter Johnson High School on a Wednesday. We held a meeting on Tuesday to discuss the game and the usual expectations of how things would progress leading up to the game. Shiotani and Armstead gave us a rundown of the lineup and what to expect, but of course we were more occupied with other thoughts. We were more focused on wondering how good Walter Johnson was. Some of our players who had played on girls varsity the previous fall season gave us a rundown of the girl players we could expect to see. Tyler and Avery were aware of the state of boys' varsity in the county and gave us some tips about boys who might be playing on coed.

When the team was not physically together, we resorted to spending a great deal of time texting each other about anything we could think of. Every moment we spent not on the court together, we spent making each other laugh and having a good time. Part of that was due to our nerves leading up to games, but it was also the nature of our team. We had free and open communication with each other, and those moments you have with people you come to know over a period of time are the real moments you remember years down the road in life.

A couple of days before the game, Noah missed practice because of some outside school-related commitments. In a typical Noah move, he sent everyone a text: "Sorry team can't make it today. Your all-star MVP striker will be back tomorrow though."

This would come to start our "fake squad" banter. We had started a fun game with each other to see who would be the first to not show up or "fake" on the team. Noah was the first one to fake. If you were branded fake, it would stick with you until you made amends for it. The only way someone could remove the title of "fake" was to play well in a game.

On Tuesday, a day before the game, we were informed that practice had been officially canceled because of harsh weather conditions. Because of our game the next day, we still held an unofficial meeting to discuss any concerns or questions. Some of the newer players on coed were not accustomed to how things were conducted, and it was important to have time to address anything which could potentially surface on game day. What was most wonderful about that day was watching Coach Shio try his hardest to keep us focused, but one after another, all we could do was make each other laugh to the point where volleyball no longer became our primary concern. For the time being, we were just happy to be together. There were mentions about a possible school closure the next day, given the weather conditions and such. It didn't faze us, because of our goofball mentality. Room 233 had become our hub of fun.

On Wednesday, March 21, 2018, I awoke to messages from everyone about school delays. It was the day of our season opener, but because of the delay at school, the game had been pushed to Thursday, the 22nd. Everyone was freaking out about it. There was so much going on that it felt like nothing was normal. Was the game still on? Why did the coaches cancel practice? When was picture day? Our group chat was bombarded with comments and concerns about a million things.

After the storm calmed, we pulled ourselves together, and Jaya called for a team meeting in which she addressed each concern. Jaya was a clear-cut leader and one we desperately needed. A team is defined by its leadership, and we were lucky to have someone like her who not only was intellectually sound in all matters of volleyball but in all aspects of life.

One important thing we discussed together was what we were going to wear for spirit for our first game of the season. Every year at Blair, coed volleyball, like most sports, decides on a team-wide attire that everyone wears the day of each game. We decided that for our game on Thursday, March 22nd, our spirit was going to be jerseys. We wanted to make a statement and represent Blair proudly.

On Thursday, the bus was scheduled to leave Blair at four p.m. We gathered outside the main gym in the hallway to sit and talk. Ariel, who was no longer playing coed, brought up the Walter Johnson coed team in conversation. Apparently, one of the players who was supposed to play on boys' varsity ended up staying on coed, which led to mass hysteria. Just when we thought things couldn't get more nerve wracking, Ariel continued by naming other players and giving us their skill levels. She gave us some tips about their habits and how to overcome or limit their strengths.

It was unusual to have an away game as a season opener. It was also more anxiety-provoking, knowing we would not have a great deal of fan support at our first game. The silver lining for away games was always the bus ride, and our first one to Walter Johnson High School was no different. It was a longer drive than usual, so it gave us time to fool around. I sat near the front of the bus with my cousin Muhammad. Tyler, Noah, Shio, and Armstead were in the front. They were occupied with their clipboards, drawing up plays and lineups and trying to prepare for every possible game scenario. I turned around to see the back half of the bus partying as they danced and sang various songs. Brenna and Olivia were leading the bus in a singing competition.

In previous seasons, bus rides would normally be quiet, with the occasional outburst of energy. Players usually isolated themselves in their music or sat quietly in an attempt to mask their anxiety. The 2017-2018 season was different. We had laughs and we weren't nervous. We were pumped up to finally be playing volleyball. Shio stood up, which signaled our arrival at Walter Johnson.

The entrance to the gym was to the right of the main entrance. Tiffany, along with some other players, had come separately and met us there. We walked in and took a flight of stairs up to the main floor. They had already set up their net, and a huge crowd was beginning to gather. As we inched our way toward our side of the court, all we could hear were the familiar sounds of any volleyball game: balls bouncing and shoes thumping across gym floors. Those sounds were ones I had been looking forward to for months. I noticed men with cameras on their shoulders walking around placing microphones and interviewing various people. I thought maybe it was because it was the first game of the season since I could not think of any other occasion.

Our game was due to start at 7:15, which meant boys varsity would go first, so we had time to watch and get mentally ready. We warmed up and captains were called. I had already told Jaya what side of the coin I was going to pick before the game. It was another little thing we started senior year. I was to call the coin toss before each game. I went with tails because tails never fail, you know, and it worked! We elected to serve.

As I was warming up along with my cousin, I could feel the excitement pumping through my body. I knew we had a strong team and I couldn't wait to play with them. The buzzer rang, signaling our turn to warm up first. You could sense the excitement in the air. The crowd was cheering for their home team. It didn't matter. We were laser-focused. We first started with passing drills, breaking up into two sets of teams to run plays more smoothly. One after another we ran down the sideline toward Coach Armstead as she tossed us a pass. "Hitting lines," she yelled as we transitioned to our individual set positions.

Jaya and Fiona, our setters, both broke up the sets, one working on the outside and the other working on the right side and middle hits. Walter Johnson watched as we got better with every ball. Slowly, we began to tap into our skillset and showcase a display they would not forget. "Serve for two minutes!" yelled Shio, and we grabbed a ball and ran to both ends of the floor. The buzzer rang signaling the end of our warm-up. Walter Johnson was next.

Shio pulled us to the stairwell outside the main gym. There was a massive window near where we stood. The sun was beginning to set, and its warm rays of light lit up our little huddle. I looked around as my teammates' faces were illuminated with a bright golden aura. Shio waited before he spoke. His voice was soft and gentle. There was no special message that needed to be said. He emphasized fundamentals and the importance of communication. We all had each other, and if we could trust each other and play as one, then no one could stop us. We put our hands together and with a thunderous voice, yelled, "Blair on three. One, two, three . . . Blair!"

We marched onto the court uplifted and ready to begin this long-awaited journey of ours.

Our sidelines were facing the bleachers, an unusual setting, and it added to the challenge of having to deal with away-game noise and distractions. We watched as Walter Johnson finished their warmups. Taking note of each player, I spoke to my team about what tendencies I could make out, and we began mapping our strategy.

The buzzer rang and it was game time.

Shio submitted his lineup, and we stood at the end line of our side. Before every match it was a show of sportsmanship for both teams to wish each other good luck by having the starting six clap each other's hands at the net. Avery, Tyler, Tiffany, Jaya, Brenna, and I, the lineup chosen by Shio and Armstead, started the match. We all stood together in our positions so the ref could verify the lineup. He gave us a thumbs up.

I called everyone together in a huddle. "Okay, guys, listen up. It's here. Our first game. Remember, communicate! I want to hear all of you talk. If you make a mistake, shake it off. If we score, celebrate. We need to be a team. Have each other's back."

As I was in the middle of my best Shio speech impression, a man walked over with a camera and started recording our huddle. I thought that was pretty strange. He seemed very focused on Brenna, so we asked her about it. Given her recent involvement with the protests and march after the high school shootings, a documentary or something like that was being made about her. We all sort of stood there and just nodded along. It did, however, take some pressure off us because we had something to sort of preoccupy our minds before the game started. The referee signaled with his hand and we broke our mini huddle with a "Blair on three" cheer.

We served first. Tiffany, with her unique run-up and deadly serving, was able to secure a point. "Ace!" we all yelled. An ace is when a player scores a point directly off a serve with the ball either hitting the floor of the court directly or if a player received it and shanks it (it goes off them and becomes unplayable).

She served again. This time they received it and set a quick ball to the outside. "Tip! Tip!" yelled Tyler as they rolled the ball over our block.

It was a constant back-and-forth battle for a while, but with their home crowd, Walter Johnson then gained some momentum and took a nice cushion lead. We were having trouble receiving their serves, and slowly, mistakes began occurring with increased frequency.

"Side-out," yelled everyone on the bench, including Shio and Armstead. In volleyball a side-out is when a team that is serving does not win the rally, losing a point and giving the other team the opportunity to serve next.

The crowd was getting more excited, and they fed off the energy. Shio called timeout and called us over. "You guys are doing good, just mental mistakes. Remember, communicate with each other and watch for those tips and rolls," he said.

We were starting to get a little nervous. We broke the huddle and resumed play. Walter Johnson continued their run. With every point, the bleachers turned into what sounded like thunder coming from afar. Walter Johnson pulled away and secured the first set.

We switched sides. Directly across our view were their sidelines. Shio pulled us into a huddle and Armstead began going over the set. She pointed out what we had done well and what had hurt us. Walter Johnson had utilized many tips and relied on our mistakes to gain many of their points. "Fix your mistakes, guys. They aren't scoring these points, you're giving it to them," said Armstead.

We broke the huddle. I called everyone together again. I raised my voice and looked each player directly in the eye. "Guys, they aren't better than us. We need to talk more. Everyone, call everything and be where you need to be. Fix your mistakes and let's take it one point at a time."

They all woke up. As I walked back to my spot, Jaya whispered, "Nice job, captain," as she smiled and walked to her position.

The second set started with Walter Johnson serving. We were able to receive their serves well, but our hitting was not quite there yet. Pulling away with a little lead, they called timeout to ice our server. When you ice a server, you essentially stop momentum in the hopes that the timeout puts pressure on the server, forcing an error. Shio again reminded us of fundamentals as Armstead was breaking down the point statistics.

We broke the huddle and served with ease. Slowly, our hitting began to improve. As Noah and Olivia subbed in, we had a consistent upfront attack. Tiffany, with her pass receive and defense, was starting to own the back end of the court. She was our libero. Tyler and Avery did Tyler and Avery things, excelling as all-around players. Jaya and Fiona subbed and rotated with each other to keep Walter Johnson off balance. We were not clicking completely as a team, but parts of our game were slowly coming together. Blair won the second set.

It was now tied at 1-1. More yelling and more fighting later, we battled our way through the third set to take a 2-1 lead. Our plays were a little more consistent, but we were not totally in sync and lost easy points by making fixable errors. Walter Johnson had tried to tip and attack our soft spots in the defense, but we adapted to their tendencies and took away their strong plays. Noah was beginning to get more comfortable near the net. He, along with Brenna, had some monster blocks to which we all yelled, "Denied!" as we mimicked their arm motions on a block.

The fourth set began with Walter Johnson running some points to take an early lead. We were aced a couple of times and had a few hitting errors. I looked over at Shio, and he signaled with his hands where to go with the ball. I pulled Noah and Olivia to the side and told them to attack Walter Johnson's weak players who were having trouble in defense. We tied it up. It was back and forth. They would ace us and we'd respond right back with our own kills.

As both teams inched their way toward the 25-point mark, something suddenly just clicked in all of us. We suddenly became inspired with energy, and our communication improved so much it was as if we had played together all our lives. Rallying off points with ease, we pulled away to win the set and the game, 3-1. As the final whistle blew, a sigh of relief left all of us. Everyone ran onto the court and hugged each other. We forgot about the post-game handshake, so we had to turn back.

Armstead and Shio pulled us aside and congratulated us. "Those last points, that's how we need to play more often. Great job, guys, let's get a Blair on three and head out," said Shio. Seeing everyone's smiles that day was truly something special to witness.

On the bus ride home, everyone went nuts. Music was played louder than ever. Shio and Armstead couldn't help but join in on the fun. But I sat in my seat, looking out the window, my mind elsewhere. Although, we had won, and played better than any game I could remember during my time at Blair, we hadn't played that great. Points had been left on the board and there were many improvements to be made.

Shio noticed my preoccupation and tapped me on the shoulder. "Great job out there today," he said.

"I know, but we didn't play that great."

He looked me in the eye, ever so clever and cool, and said, "Don't worry about it. Enjoy today and rest up. We got Sherwood next."

Chapter 13

One Can Only Dream

I walked into the gym on the Friday after the game. It was our last practice before spring break. Some players were already sitting against the wall, waiting for Shio to open the equipment room. We all changed and passed the ball around. Everyone was excited about the win the day before, and rightfully so. There were a lot of positives to be happy about but also many mistakes we had to work on. The rest of our schedule came up in conversation. We took a peek at the schedule, and to our collective disbelief, our next opponent was Sherwood High School. They had owned Blair the last couple of years.

We always played them early on in the year, most of the time as the season opener, but for the 2017-2018 season, we had a little playing experience heading into Sherwood. I had talked to Shio about why the schedule was like that. He explained that, with a team like Sherwood, playing them early was no good because we had not glued together as a team yet. We had to make do with whatever the situation was and go with it.

Time passed and more players slowly entered the gym. Shio walked in carrying his duffle bag over his shoulder with a key in his hand. He looked focused. His usual smile was absent. With a force behind his voice, he announced across the gym, "Everyone, get dressed, and let's get the net set up quickly."

Setting up the net was always like our little tea time before practice. As a team we always talked about our day at school or anything happening in our lives. As you walked down the gym hallway, to your left was the equipment room. For some reason our nets and volleyballs were always behind the gymnastics equipment. They had this huge mat that was set up on a rolling system, blocking our ball bags. The poles were always behind the door and were extremely heavy! I would opt for taking the ball bags while the big boys took the two poles. Being a captain has its benefits, I must say.

We set up the net and got dressed. Before warmups, Shio called us over to the wall where the exit was. We gathered in a semicircle around him. He again congratulated us on our win but then immediately followed it by asking us to forget it. "That game is over. Now it's on to the next one. We got Sherwood after the break. We won't have practice over the next week, so everyone needs to be on their A-game today," he said.

In our time together, we had always lost to Sherwood in straight sets. Every year they always had better players and more experience. This year, for once, we had a legitimate shot at beating them, but our schedule gave us a huge disadvantage. Friday practice was our only official team practice before spring break. The Sherwood game was scheduled for Wednesday, April 4, 2018, which gave us only two more practices before the game.

As an athlete, practice is such an important part of sports, and not having it for a week can lead to significant consequences for a team. The only option we had over break was to continue with our own home practices, but it was important for us to build team chemistry and learn how to play together, which required team practices.

We broke the huddle and were off to peppering. Everyone was focused. There wasn't much laughter, which was not normal for a Friday practice. Sherwood was the one team we circled on our calendars. Armstead decided to conduct practice a little differently.

Rather than running our usual schedule of drills, she decided to do conditioning before our volleyball-related workouts. "Alright, everyone, we're going to be working on conditioning," she said as we all sighed with disbelief.

Everyone whispered to each other, questioning her decision, but we had no choice but to do the workouts. Otherwise, running ladders was our only other option. Running ladders meant starting at one end of the volleyball court and running back and forth between each attack and midline, as well as the net line, until we ran the entire court. It is a grueling exercise and one volleyball players dread.

Coach Armstead set up cones to divide the floor into zones. Each zone was for working on a different part of the body. One area was for core workouts. Armstead had us sit against a wall for a minute straight, a 30-second break, and then another minute. After that series, she whistled and we rotated to the next zone, which emphasized jumping. We faced the wall and picked a spot that was our highest jumping point. For an entire minute straight, all we did was jump up and down. Another whistle blew and we moved to the next drill to work on floor movement. Cones had been set up around the floor, and the goal was to shuffle between cones as quickly as possible. Hitting drills were changed. Instead of using a volleyball, we used tennis balls to work on wrist snapping to increase our hitting power. It felt strange at first. We kept throwing the tennis balls into the net, thinking they were going over when they were only going through. Passers worked in sets of two to complete 50 passes on both knees. Everyone was sweating, and it was one of the hardest practices we'd ever had. That day of practice was filled with the sounds of people gasping for air. Finally, Armstead whistled, concluding conditioning. We all went for a sip of water and watched the boys practice, as we had some time to kill.

Coach Chris was on the sidelines, wearing his usual attire of a hoodie with loose joggers, a bottle of soda in one hand. During breaks, I went over and chatted with him about the boys team. He always teased me for stealing away Tyler and Avery.

During one break, as we were talking, Shio signaled me over. The team gathered around as he and Armstead introduced some new concepts they wanted us to learn. For the most part we had run a basic rotational scheme with standard plays. The usual pass, set, and hit type of plays. Shio wanted us to learn some new sets, as well as defensive positions, to counter common errors we'd made in our previous game. For one, we needed to work more with middle defense. Tipping and middle attacks were killing us, and so we instituted a defense in which we would form a sort of semi-circle around the middle, ensuring all parts of the court were covered. Jaya and Fiona started setting newer types of plays, mostly quick sets, which we didn't run much, and fake attacks.

Sherwood was strong in everything they did. All their players were experienced and skilled, so we needed to up our game both physically and schematically.

Practice concluded with an ab workout, which we all hated. As we came in for a final huddle, Shio reminded us to stay hydrated through the week, to watch our diet, and to stay away from anything that could injure us (as he stared directly at Tyler, who was known for being injury prone).

—⁂—

Over spring break the team and I went back and forth about random things. Yearbook writers from Blair asked us to provide some information and images of coed volleyball. Ariel sent us an old video from the previous year. What became known as the most famous volleyball memory at Blair was our go-to video when we needed to laugh about something: the iconic "Avery Face Receive" was during the 2016-2017 season in a game against Richard Montgomery when a player from the opposing boys varsity team hit a ball directly into Avery's face. Moments like that live on through the years and still circulate the volleyball spheres at Blair.

On March 30, 2018, at 4:35 p.m., Jaya started a conversation in our group chat about our upcoming divisional games. She asked:

Which teams are in our division?

In our division, called the Gold Division, the teams included Blair, Einstein, Kennedy (John F Kennedy), Wheaton, Rockville, and Northwood high schools. The way the schedule was set up made it so that all division games were in a row. If you missed one game, then chances were you had already lost your shot at winning the division. That year our first three games were all non-division games. Then immediately after, we had our five division games. It was weird that Jaya was asking about divisional opponents; I knew she had played in prior years. But then she hit the team with a curve ball. She asked us plain and simple regarding the division games,

"Which one do you prefer I miss?"

We all reacted with a bunch of "Whoas" and "Whats."

I responded jokingly with, "**Kennedy.**"

Tyler texted: "**U can miss all of them if you want :).**"

We then had a real conversation about it. Jaya missing a game became our primary concern. I thought, *Well, Northwood won't really matter, Einstein is important, Rockville won the division the last three years, Wheaton is an unknown, and we already beat Kennedy in the pre-season, so Kennedy is a good choice.*

Jaya threw another curveball: "Well technically I'm missing 3." Jaya had a number of college visits and important senior-related things to attend to.

I wish I could have seen everyone's reaction to those words in person. Luckily, we had Fiona, but losing Jaya meant losing a crucial part of our leadership.

—⚘—

A day before the Sherwood game we went over our spirit attire, which had always been jerseys for away games. Olivia—Liv as we called her—with her childlike personality, chimed in and asked who and where we were playing. Sherwood wasn't the answer she expected.

Armstead sent out an email about coaches coming late. She instructed us to set up and do a pre-workout without any volleyballs. Of course that was exactly the opposite of what we did. In true Blair fashion, we messed around and just talked when we should have been practicing. As the coaches walked in, we put on our best Oscar performances to make it look like we were hard at work. Shio probably knew we hadn't been doing anything, but he kept quiet.

Our practice was intense that day but in a controlled manner. To avoid injuries or overdoing anything, we stuck to our fundamentals and kept things relatively simple. With an opponent like Sherwood, Shio knew it would be easy for us to get caught up in the moment and overdo things that could lead to careless mistakes. I huddled the team before we ended practice to speak with them about the game. This was Blair's chance to knock off the king of the county. I told them about the rivalry between Blair and Sherwood from the previous two years, with coed specifically. Although Sherwood was not a real rival in the context of our division, they were always the game of the year for us. Shio, Brenna, and I really wanted to beat them. We broke the huddle to Tyler's "Blair on three" cheer.

On Wednesday, April 4, 2018, we arrived at Sherwood. As we drove on the main road, the school appeared to our left. I remember being overwhelmed by how massive it was. It felt like a college campus. They had a huge, beautiful back yard with various sporting venues, and their football field, which was to the left, immediately caught everyone's attention. As we pulled up to the gym entrance, we could already see droplets of blue entering the school. Our dark reds were a stark contrast to theirs and caught the attention of everyone as we made our way to the gym.

We walked into their gym, and I remember the music playing really loudly. It was hard to hear anyone. You literally had to be standing next to someone in order for them to hear you. The ceiling was lower than ours, not to mention the fact that there was a rope that ran across right on top of the net.

It was another 7:15 game, which meant Sherwood would have a nice home crowd by the end of the night as students trickled into the gym after their respective sports practices. The night games in volleyball are the equivalent of Friday Night Lights in football, not to the exact same extent, but they are the highlight of the games during volleyball season.

Warmups went normally and captains were called. Blair won the coin toss again with my pregame decision ritual, and we elected to serve. I watched as they warmed up. They looked perfect. Their hitting was not only powerful, but their passing and defense were unfazed by anything thrown at them. Their serves were all consistent and they had depth on their roster. We knew it was going to be a tough game.

Shio submitted his lineup and pulled us aside for a talk. He stressed the importance of playing Blair volleyball and not getting caught up in the fact that we were playing Sherwood. "Focus on fundamentals," he said. "Be where you need to be and don't worry about the scoreboard," he added with his iconic Shio smile.

As we stood in our positions, Jaya, Tyler, Avery, Brenna, Tiffany, and I all looked at each other with smiles on our faces. I called them in for a mini huddle and put on my captain hat again. "Listen up, guys. Don't worry about them. Let's worry about us. Everyone talk to each other and be loud. We need to keep our balls in and minimize our mistakes." We put our hands together, this time using both hands. We looked at each other and yelled, breaking our huddle.

We served over and they received it with ease. Their setter set the outside, and a thunderous hit later, we were down by one. Sherwood dominated the entire set with ease. We fought back, closing the gap toward the end, but they pulled away and won the first set.

The second set was no different. Sherwood took the early lead. Our mental mistakes cost us a lot of points. At times we made it a good fight, but Sherwood would recapture the momentum and use it to propel them to a greater lead. They won the second set, making it 2-0.

On the third set, we were tired and out of it. Our communication had lessened and our play was starting to break down. We barely held on and were swept clean, 3 sets to 0.

It was a devastating loss. At the time, even though we were only two games into the season, it felt as if we had already lost it all. If our team wasn't able to beat Sherwood, then how would we ever take the championship?

The bus ride back to school was silent. Everyone was either looking out the window or tired, their eyes closed. I sat looking out the window, pondering about the rest of the season. This had been my fear from the start, and it needed to change. We had the talent but weren't playing to our potential. I moved to sit across from Shio. We spoke the entire ride back. In times like these, I often turned to him for guidance and help. He knew me better than most and had a way of looking at the bright side of things, even when it seemed as though there was no hope. His smile and radiant personality kept my hopes up. "Don't worry about today. We'll see them in the play-offs," he said.

I hoped he was right. But for the time being, it was on to the next game.

Chapter 14

All We've Been Through

As I recall my three years with Coach Shio, our paths were an unlikely crossing, but the sport of volleyball brought us together in a cool way. Elliott Shiotani was a math teacher at Montgomery Blair High School. He was also the Blair field hockey head coach. While at Blair, I had never heard of or known anyone named Shiotani prior to meeting him in my sophomore year. I would later find out that I crossed his classroom every day on my way to my math class.

Shio is a very relaxed and positive person. When you meet him for the first time, you get the impression that he is a very relatable guy. He loves to eat candy and wear flannel shirts. His round face and messy haircut give off a warm and funny personality. His jokes and humor always lighten the mood, and he knows how to connect with people.

When I first met Shio, we were complete strangers, but as time went on we developed a close bond that became the foundation of coed volleyball. Shio never got angry or yelled at us during practice or games. He always kept calm, and whatever happened, he never stopped smiling. Sometimes, during games, I would tease him about jump serving, and he always threatened to bench me if I did. Shio had this aura about him where he somehow knew exactly how to get the best out of us. If we ever had a 3-0 win, Shio made us run and practice even harder the next day. At first we were confused as to why he made that choice. Normally, coaches gave their players rest the day after a game, but Shio knew how to keep the standards high, not only when it came to our athletic lives but in everything, be it in school or outside school. He always stressed taking care of our health and taking our education seriously. If anyone needed any help, he always offered whatever help he could, and he always imparted whatever wisdom he had to us, not to mention his hilarious stories.

During both lunch periods at Blair, the mathematics department held its tutoring services in Shio's classroom, and I was one of the volunteers who helped him as part of the bliss tutoring program. I only knew Shio from a player's perspective for two years, given that was the extent of our relationship, but in my senior year of high school, I learned about Elliott Shiotani off the court and away from volleyball. I got to see a vulnerable side to him. Students of all types and from all levels of classes came to his classroom for help during lunch periods, and he made an effort to help all of them, regardless of who they were. Their improved understanding and ability with math were a true testament to his ability as a teacher and mentor.

I remember one particular incident on a bus ride after our first season together. I was feeling pretty down about everything. We had only won a couple of games, and very little progress was being made. Shio sat next to me and we talked for however long the ride was. He told me about his time with field hockey and how there were ups and downs, both during the season and from year to year. He taught me the importance of always working hard and never worrying too much about results or awards, that it was the process of whatever it is you love doing that was the priority. That was who Shio was. He wasn't the pregame hype coach or the yelling type of motivator, nor was he a strategic mastermind. He knew exactly what to say, when to say it, and how—with a smile on his face. Our coed volleyball seasons would not have been fun without Shio, not to mention the fact that we would not have had the success we did. Every athlete has a coach in their life that is held in more special regard than others. For me, it was the down-to-earth guy in room 233, wearing a flannel shirt and eating candy with a smile on his face.

Coach Shio

Chapter 15

The Sweeps So Clean

With the way our coed volleyball schedules were set up, multiple games could occur within one week, sometimes as many as three. It so happened that two days after the Sherwood game, we had another game, this one against Poolesville High School. That was an important game because not only was it a bounce-back game, but Jaya would not be present. When I arrived home after the Sherwood loss, I texted the group chat: "Bad that we lost today but bounce back on Friday for Poolesville."

As a captain, now that Jaya was missing a game, I had to step up and fill her shoes as best as I could. If we wanted to reach our goals for the year, we had to step up our game, and it started with me.

Practice the day before the Poolesville game was one of the most unique ones ever instituted during my time at Blair. Shio and Armstead decided to strip away the volleyball stuff and focus on team building and chemistry. Armstead had us cover our mouths so we couldn't communicate verbally. We also tied our arms together and locked them in a passing position. At first it was extremely difficult to practice. As volleyball players can tell you, playing without freedom of movement or talking is taking away the two most important elements of any player's game. It was extremely uncomfortable as well, but it greatly improved our skills.

We ran normal drills the whole day in that condition. I also vividly remember gaining a new appreciation for volleyball.

Oftentimes, as athletes we can become so focused on external goals that we forget to cherish the fact that we have the ability and means to even play sports to begin with. I had not realized how great a blessing talking and movement were until that day in practice. It elevated my love for the sport and in a way humbled me into a more disciplined state. I remember various students from other sports walking into the gym and looking over at us with their phones out. We looked stupid for sure, but it was necessary for team bonding. We knew we had talent, but we hadn't been playing as a cohesive unit yet. Division games were coming up after Poolesville, so we had to be ready.

Before practice ended, Shio had us run a scrimmage game without the tape and rope to see how much progress we had made. We ran a six v six game among ourselves. Jaya would not be playing on Friday, so she switched to the other team, while Fiona was with the starters. My cousin served the ball over, and as soon as his hand made contact with the ball, all six of us starters began calling everything we were seeing.

"Balls up, balls up," we yelled as it came over the net.

"I got it, I got it!" yelled Tyler as he passed a perfect ball to Fiona, who set Liv with a pass.

Liv struck the ball with a thunderous force, and right down the line it went through three players. Play after play we began talking and yelling more. We were finally beginning to scratch the surface of what it meant to truly play as a team.

It was hard to explain being in that moment. It felt almost like we had some sort of telepathic connection with each other and could communicate our next moves without even looking at where everyone was on the court.

Volleyball is a sport that requires a heightened sense of understanding and awareness about your moment-to-moment subjective experience. The sport forces you to look at everything happening in relation to yourself and the ball. As you gather information about the ball in real time, you are unconsciously planning future movements. As a team, when you can play like that, you become unstoppable. We ended practice on a high note with a strong kill from Noah in the middle and went over last-minute game preparations. The Poolesville game was our first home game, so we decided to go with formal attire for spirit wear.

Friday, April 6, 2018, the day of the Poolesville game, we got the news that Ms. Boule was going to attend the match. Ms. Boule was the head of the athletic department at Blair. She is an extremely kind person and one of the most passionate when it comes to sports. She loved coed volleyball—she admitted it was her favorite sport—and had much faith in us becoming a successful program at Blair. One of her dreams was to have Blair win something for coed because it was one of the few sports at Blair that had an empty poster in the main gym.

Each sport had a poster on the wall in the main gym showcasing the years that sport had won either division or county or whatever major award they had won. As you looked around, you saw sports with multiple wins in multiple categories. Boys' varsity had wins in both division and county. And then there was coed volleyball. Their poster was as empty as a clean sheet of copy paper.

Noah asked if there was a playlist for games and pregame warmups. We didn't have an official playlist, but I assured him that it would be taken care of. Blair had a speaker system with an auxiliary cord, so you can probably guess what song started the pregame warmups. Team photos for coed were also scheduled in the small gym the day of the Poolesville game. The plan was to head to Four Corners, grab lunch, and meet up in the small gym, ready for pictures. Four Corners is the local shopping district right in front of Blair at the intersection of University Boulevard and Colesville Road. The coed team was always split between Chipotle, Subway, and Santucci's. We grabbed our lunch and headed back to school.

Pictures were something we always struggled with. We never could stop giggling, and the smallest things could set us off on a laughing spree. The photographer would stand there counting down, and then all of a sudden we would burst out in laughter. It sort of started to hit us seniors, in particular, that it was our last year ever playing volleyball for Blair. We were graduating at the end of the year, and no one was continuing their volleyball career.

First came the general team photo. We all tried to purposefully make each other laugh or do funny faces, but Shio made us stop. Then came the senior photos. We lined up on the bleachers. On the bottom row were Noah, Tyler, Avery, and me. Above us were Brenna, Tiffany, and Jaya. I tried my best to smile, but I was distracted by the underclassmen in the background dancing or making funny gestures. We then finished up with solo shoots. Pictures were never something we had enjoyed before the 2017-2018 season. It was one of the things we dreaded doing but was required by the school. But that year was different. We made it an unforgettable experience and one that would last our lifetimes.

For the Poolesville game, boy's varsity went first, so we watched while some of us worked as line judges or with the scoreboard. Shio told us to start warmups after the second set to get ready and save time on the clock for when we had to go. As the final whistle blew for the boy's game, we all marched onto the floor and began our usual routine. As everyone was peppering with each other, I quickly ran over and grabbed my phone. I asked Ms. Boule for the auxiliary cord and started "God's Plan" by Drake. The speakers were at full volume. It was quiet in the gym and then all of a sudden, the room became filled with energy as the lyrics started on the speakers. Everyone on the court, including the Poolesville players, sang along. People in the stands sang along too. I looked over and saw Noah pumping his head to the beat. His eyes locked on me, and he gave me two thumbs up.

Montgomery Blair Highschool coed volleyball 2017-2018 team photo. From left to right: Coach Shiotani, Olivia, Noah, Brenna, Sarah, Coach Armstead, Mizan, Edward, Me, Tyler, Avery, River, Fiona, Isabelle, Ruben, Abby, Tiffany, Muhammad, Elisabeth, and Jaya.

Captains were called. I had already told Fi what I was going to pick, and somehow, we won the coin toss for a third straight time! We elected to serve. Shio submitted his lineups and gave us his smile before the game. Ms. Boule was in the stands. along with some families, like Tyler's Dad, Liv's younger sister and parents, and friends we all knew.

It was our first home game, so I called the starting six together. "Alright, guys, first home game. Remember what we learned in practice, communicate and help each other out. Call everything you see and be where you need to be. I'm pretty sure no one wants to wear tape over their mouths again," I said as they all laughed. I pulled Fiona aside and told them not to worry too much about anything. They were the floor general, so if they wanted us to be in a certain position or make a change, Fiona had free rein to do whatever they felt was best.

The whistle blew and Fiona served a powerful knuckleball. "Ace!" we all yelled as it hit the floor between two Poolesville players. Fi went on to score a couple more aces before Poolesville earned back a point. This time there was no back and forth. Blair was in control from start to finish. Not only were we talking, but our play was smooth and we were scoring points off kills as opposed to relying on the other team's mistakes. Our defensive transitions were perfect and we rarely made any mental mistakes. We won the first set easily to go up 1-0.

The second set was no different. We played smoothly, and our chemistry improved even more. Noah and Brenna were controlling the middle. They were blocking Poolesville's attacks, and any that went over or were tipped were dug up by Tyler or Tiffany. Fiona was setting with ease, and my kills were becoming more consistent. We won the second and third sets to secure a 3-0 win.

As the final whistle rang, we all jumped in celebration. Everyone hugged each other, the bleachers went crazy, and Ms. Boule gave us a thumbs up. In our excitement we huddled up near the exit of the gym hallway and couldn't control our smiles. Shio and Armstead did their best to go over the game and congratulate us, but even they couldn't hold back their smiles. As we broke the huddle and walked to take down the nets, Shio pulled me aside and said, "That's how you need to play."

I drove home that night and opened my phone to a bombardment of messages on our group chat.

"**3-0 solid,**" Tiffany texted, letting Jaya know we won. Elisabeth, River, Jaya, Liv, and Noah all chimed in with congrats and warm appraisals. The highlight of the game was Noah's block. When it happened we all screamed the loudest we had ever screamed in a game up to that point in time. That win felt really nice. It wasn't just that we won 3-0, it was how we played. We were finally starting to click as a team. But there was still a great deal of room for improvement. That game was a much-needed win because the next five games were division games. We celebrated our victory, but we knew Saturday would be the start of the real test.

Chapter 16

The Hard-Earned Dues

After the game on Friday, April 7, just as I was preparing to go to bed, I received a notification from Coach Armstead. I was immediately drawn to the words "Saturday Practice" painted across the screen, and like anyone who was looking forward to the weekend, I threw back my head and yelled as loud as I could into my pillow. She had mentioned something about it earlier in the year, but I never thought she was serious about it.

As soon as that notification was sent, everyone on the team went haywire. "Wait, so Saturday practice for sure?" asked Avery. This was at 12:22 in the morning, mind you. Practice was scheduled to start between 8:00 to 8:30 a.m. We talked for an hour or more when we should have been getting some rest, given practice was that same morning.

Not everyone could make it, and some even tried to not come, but when Armstead offered to bring donuts, the turnout magically increased.

I arrived in the student parking lot along with my cousin Muhammad. We were surprised to see how many cars were there. Unbeknownst to us, nearly every spring sport was holding a Saturday practice. Because of the recent delays and school closures, the spring schedule had to be shrunk a little more, which meant less practice during the season. It was the first time that official weekend practices were held at Blair in my memory. The thought of Saturday practice at first was not a very pleasant one, but it was actually really fun. For once we didn't have to worry about school that day, and for the most part, the entire building was empty.

We all met at the front entrance. Armstead was there with two boxes of donuts to which all of our eyes were glued. We walked in to find that the hallways were very dark. Few lights were on, and it felt like walking into some kind of haunted house. It was totally silent. Every word we uttered, no matter how faint, could be heard. We quickly set up the nets and began doing some drills. Armstead wanted us to work more on individual skills rather than having general practice drills. That way we could focus more on our individual weaknesses. I was at the net, working on blocking. Noah was with Fiona, working on his approaches and hitting. Other players were working on passing and defense. We were also able to run some scrimmage games and really break down defensive schemes with more depth.

In volleyball the offensive part of the game is not as complicated as the defense. You'll often hear that old saying, "Defense wins championships." That is 100 percent true in the sport of volleyball. Everything starts with defense.

Armstead had us bring her some boxes in from the school gym which were mainly used for jumping exercises. She placed them in hitting positions and stood on them. That way she could simulate a consistent and strong offensive attack from various positions. Our job was to transition to base defense and just practice receiving various hits. It was extremely annoying because Armstead would purposely give us very strange hits that confused us. I didn't realize it at the time, but she was preparing us for every possible scenario and forcing us to really pay attention to the art of reading a hitter's body language and reacting accordingly.

On one particular occasion she ran a play similar to what Walter Johnson High School had run that won them the first set during our season opener. As opposed to going for a full-on spike, the outside hitter would roll or tip the ball to their right and have it land between the middle, our outside hitter, and left back. That play confused us greatly and we all sort of looked at each other, not knowing whose ball it was.

Our problem was our lack of communication. As opposed to talking to each other and figuring out who was responsible for that ball, we just watched as it fell. We decided that the outside hitter needed to be ready to transition for a hit, so it didn't make much sense for them to get it. The middle blocker appeared to be the closest player, but they had to run backward, and chances were they wouldn't be as fast to make it compared to the left back, who had a straight-line angle at the ball. Slowly, our understanding of the game was getting better.

We ran some more sets and finished practice with a friendly game and headed home.

Chapter 17

In the End, You Kept Me Going

On Sunday after our first-ever Saturday practice, we discussed our upcoming divisional games. The schedule had us playing two games that coming week, on Monday and Friday, followed by a three-game week to finish out division matches. Monday was a half day, so our pregame preparations were a little bit different.

I texted the team:

> "The next five games are division games. So everyone needs to be on there A game."

Of course, I realized I wrote "there" instead of "their," but thankfully, no one noticed. I focused a great deal on those next five games because I knew they were our last chance as seniors to win a division title. Seniors would graduate and there would be no guarantees the following year.

The first game scheduled was against Albert Einstein High School (or just Einstein as we called them). At the time they were undefeated, winning all their games in straight sets, so we knew it wouldn't be an easy outing. It was also an away game for us, so Einstein would have the added benefit of home-court advantage.

Monday, April 9, 2018, the day of the Einstein game, we were eager for the school day to end as we went through our half-day schedules. Jaya would not be available for the game. Noah asked the group if there was anything planned after school because he wanted to work on hitting. Fiona was available for a little practice, so they worked with Noah, and they went over their approaches and sets. We all talked for a while and warmed up to keep our bodies loose.

The hours before games are a golden opportunity time. Usually, players feel the intense anxiety of game day or are anxious about how they are going to play, but I always found it to be a really peaceful time. Everyone had their way of pumping themselves up, but I always did the opposite. I did whatever I could to stay relaxed, so I often played to easy-listening music or meditated if possible. Coldplay is my favorite band and my go-to playlist for pregame warmups. Something about pregame hype didn't sit well for me when it came to volleyball. Unlike other sports, volleyball is not one where you necessarily need to be hyped before a game; in fact, that outpouring of emotion may end up hurting you as opposed to helping you. Staying calm is key, not only for the mental side of the game but also to keep your body physically relaxed and loose.

Another thing I often did was go over possible scenarios that could occur during games. I would think about how I would react if they had a certain type of serve that was particularly powerful, if they had a hitter who was consistently hitting, or just about anything I could think of to be as prepared as possible and, more importantly, how I would feel and play on the court.

Elisabeth called us over to Room 2, which was the digital art room. Everyone met there before the bus arrived to just hang out and talk. The bus arrived around 4:30. Noah drove my cousin and me to the game while most of the other players took the bus. We put on "God's Plan" while driving at times alongside the bus.

We arrived at Einstein and pulled into their parking lot. It was very quiet and no one was outside. I remember stepping outside the car and having a strong feeling suddenly hit me in the face. This was our last chance to win our division, and it started with this first game. Sure, Einstein was undefeated, but it would only make the win that much more amazing if we could pull it off.

Their gym was similar to Kennedy's except their ceiling was higher. We walked in to the sound of volleyballs bouncing, hitting lines progressing, and a song playing on full volume. The coed team players, along with boys' varsity, were scattered about. They all seemed very relaxed and ready for the game.

Our bleachers were right next to the entrance. I unpacked my things near the top of the bleachers next to River, who is one of the most enthusiastic and joyful people I have ever met. As we waited for our game, I felt a tap on my shoulder. River had pulled a laptop out of her bag. "Wanna play *Smash*?" she asked. Both of us were lovers of gaming and had gone back and forth about who was the better *Super Smash Brothers* player (a very famous game that was first released on Nintendo's GameCube console). Little did I know that River was a much better player than I was, as she competed in many competitive leagues and tournaments while I stayed home playing against cousins who only played for fun. Without getting too specific, let's just say River won easily, and I would no longer question who the better player was. Shio walked into the gym and saw River and me really focused on the laptop screen. He looked over and saw our controllers and just laughed as he walked away.

Boys' varsity went first, so we had time to kill. Tyler fell asleep near me, which was always a big no-no on coed. We made sure to post his snoozed face all over our Snapchat stories. Noah, my cousin, and I sat together, talking about the boys game. Everyone was scattered about. As the boy's game neared the end, Einstein's coed players arrived wearing their uniforms. The only players present prior to their arrival were working on the boy's game.

The coed players all had determined looks on their faces. They weren't there to mess around; they meant business. We watched as they gathered near their bleachers. Liv, Tiffany, Fiona, and other girls' varsity players were giving our team a rundown of who they knew from the Einstein coed team. Noah simply shrugged his shoulders, and in true Noah fashion, said, "They don't have me."

We went to warm up in a small hallway outside the gym while we waited for the boys game to end. When we heard the final whistle, we jogged back into the gym. As always, the music was loud and both teams warmed up, one on either side of the net. Captains were called, so Fiona and I walked over. Einstein's setter, who was really tall, was an experienced player who had been in the program for a long time among other players who were very good all-rotation players. I told Fiona what to call, and we won the coin toss again for a fourth straight time! Captains shook hands and back we went to our sides.

As Einstein warmed up after us we could see from their style of play that they were a legit team. The setter had a strong rapport with her hitters, and their hitting was very consistent and powerful. They had tall players and talent at every position. We noticed that the music they chose was very loud and exciting for when they were on the court. While we were warming up, they were playing country music. It didn't really bother us but, instead, made us laugh and more determined to win. *Oh, it's on!*

Some players, whose names I won't mention, didn't take that gesture too well. The final pregame buzzer rang and it was time to line up for the handshake. Before we proceeded, Shio called everyone together. Having had experience with significant division play at Blair, he knew exactly how those types of games felt for players, so he stressed staying calm and not letting Einstein's record bother us.

As he spoke, I happened to turn to the bleachers and see some parents scattered about. The one that caught my eye was Mr. Bowen Fong, Tyler's dad. He was a regular attendee for volleyball games at Blair and had come to every one of our games that year. I didn't know him that well, but I had spoken to him a few times before and after games. I snapped back into Shio's speech and we were off.

We shook hands with the Einstein players only to receive very cold looks from them. The pot was slowly brewing. Lining up in our positions for the ref to check us, I looked at Shio and told him to not worry. He was standing and looked more focused than usual. The ref gave us a thumbs up and I called everyone in for a mini huddle.

Fiona was our setter that day, so I looked at them first. Everything we did would revolve around them, so I stressed making sure our passes were perfect for them. I told hitters to keep their hits in and not do anything fancy. "Don't forget to communicate, talk to each other, and let's go out there and show them what Blair is made of," I said and we screamed, "Blair on three."

Fiona served first. Einstein received the ball and set a quick outside hit. They scored in a matter of seconds. They served over and we responded. For the first couple of points, it was a back-and-forth of kills and serving errors. Einstein flipped the switch and took off from there. Their defense adjusted to our hitting, and their setter started to dump the ball at times, catching us off guard. A dump is when a volleyball is purposefully sent over to the other side of the net as opposed to being set for a hit. If practiced enough, it can be a deadly and effective way of earning points. What adds to its effectiveness is its unpredictability. Given how Einstein's offense was playing, we had trouble on defense because of the added element of setter dumps. If we committed to hitters, it would leave spots on the court open for dumps and vice versa. One point after another, Einstein rode their momentum to win the first set and go up 1-0.

Our nerves were starting to get the better of us and Shio could see it. He and Armstead quickly went over their notes and highlighted our key mistakes. We were not getting set properly on defense, not adjusting our communication, and those setter dumps were killing us. Hitting wasn't very good and we were making simple mistakes. Before the second set started, I happened to look over at Mr. Fong sitting in the stands. He wore a blue button-down shirt and had his arms crossed. He put his hands together to create a funnel in front of his mouth and yelled, "Don't worry, Blair, you got this."

To this day I cannot explain what transpired after Mr. Fong began cheering us on. I'm not sure if there's a real switch that people can turn on or off when it comes to sports, but something triggered our switch and we weren't the same team afterwards. We instantly became filled with energy and inspiration. It was a turning point for that game and the rest of the season.

Einstein served over, I passed the ball to Fi as they set Olivia, who proceeded to get a direct kill between two Einstein players. We rallied off more points before they responded. On defense we completely shut off their front attack. Their hits were either blocked by Noah and Brenna or received by Avery, Tyler, Tiffany, or me. I started to notice Einstein's setter getting really upset and slowly losing her temper. We continued to dominate and won the set to tie it up at 1-1.

The third set was no different. Einstein could not stop our hitting attack. I was on the same page with Fi the whole day, racking up kills along with Noah, Olivia, and Brenna. Our serve receiving was better in that set than any other set we had played. We were talking more and anticipating each other's every move. On one particular play toward the end of the third set, Einstein served a ball just near our sideline toward the Blair bench. As it knuckled, I watched it all the way through just barely going out. I could see Shio's reaction and I laughed a little while assuring him I had been following it the whole time. We finished out the set, taking a 2-1 lead in the game.

The fourth set was a much more intense one. Einstein picked up some home-court momentum as they got their crowd into it, but it didn't even faze us. Throughout the game I was secretly doing something I had mentioned earlier when I was in my room one summer day. Throughout the game, I noticed Einstein's setter would get really angry at mistakes or upset about calls being made by the referee, so I told everyone on the court to target her area specifically. I instructed them that no matter what play it was, always try to aim her way. Another thing we did was every time we were near the net, in order to confuse the Einstein defense, we talked among ourselves and acted as though we were giving up where we were going to go with our next hit. Slowly, they began to unravel, and in the fourth set the setter got so angry at one point that she hurled a volleyball over the net at one of our players, nearly hitting Avery. The ref saw it and gave her a yellow card. (A yellow card is a warning for unsportsmanlike conduct.) She wasn't too happy about that.

We fought our way to a big lead. Their setter dumps were no longer working, and each of our passes was followed by a strong kill. In one particular play, everything came together beautifully. I was in the left-back position, and that play we had practiced on Saturday to help out with tips came in handy. Einstein's outside hitter tipped a ball between our middle, outside, and left-back position. It was too far for me to get it with both hands, so I ran full speed and dove with one arm out. I swung the ball upwards in the hopes that I could at least put in near Fiona. Somehow, it ended up being a perfect pass to Fiona, who set Olivia up for an easy kill.

The Einstein players froze in disbelief, their bench and bleachers suddenly quiet. Shio had his hands over his head and was also in disbelief. We all were shocked too! We had never executed such a play before. Something was clicking in all of us, and we finally began to play holistic volleyball in a truly beautiful way. Finishing up the last couple of points, we won the set and the game, 3-1, a comeback against the previously undefeated Number 1 seed in the division and county.

When the final whistle blew, everyone was ecstatic. We all ran to each other, hugging and clapping. Noah let out his screams and everyone followed. We huddled up, and Shio and Armstead, with huge grins, yelled, "Great job, everyone. That was the best we've seen you guys play all year!"

As I walked to get my stuff from the bleachers, I passed by Mr. Fong. "Nice job out there, Aziz," he said.

"Thanks" I responded.

He may not have known it at

Mr. Bowen Fong

the time, but he was the spark for us that day. After that first set, our sidelines and bleachers went cold, but he never stopped yelling and cheering us on. He always pushed us and motivated us. When we needed hope, he was there to deliver it.

The cheers continued all the way back to school. The bus ride home was like a party on wheels. In the back the speakers were blasting music. Everyone was happy, enjoying the moment. As I sat in my usual seat next to the window, I felt an overwhelming sense of relief. Part one was over. There was still work to be done, but that day felt different. It was more than just our style of play or how we won, it was our love and passion for the game that really showed on the court. Volleyball for us that game became more than just a sport to pass the time, it became a source of pure joy, and we were finally happy doing what we loved to do without having to worry about the final scoresheet.

Shio came over and congratulated me. "Feels good, doesn't it?" he asked and I nodded. "We're not finished yet. Rest up because we have another game this week. One way or another, we're getting that division trophy," he added, smiling.

Chapter 18

My Heart and Soul Continually Growing

The morning after the game, our win was all over the news at Blair. Mrs. Johnson, our principal, and the Blair athletics Twitter page retweeted our win against previously undefeated Einstein.

With emotions running high, it is very easy to come off a huge win like that only to come up short the next game. With such an important win, I knew the celebrations that would follow could either be of benefit to us or hinder our season-long objectives. It was important that we find a balance between enjoying our successes but also understanding where we wanted to be and maintaining our focus on the next game.

After the Einstein game, I took some time away to really reflect on the season we were having thus far. We were 3-1 and riding high. Normally at that point during my first two years of coed, we were either 0-4 or lucky enough to have one win. We had come such a long way from where we started, me especially. I started out not knowing much about volleyball. I had already been a captain for two years, but I never felt like a captain. Now I was much more mature, and once I began to truly understand my role as a captain, I could grow and appreciate another dimension to sports. Jaya being absent from those two games also had a significant effect: I had to step up and be a leader on the floor.

Volleyball games can be long and exhausting, especially when two teams go back and forth for a while. Momentum is usually very high early on, but over time it becomes much more difficult to maintain intensity, which can spell disaster. A captain needs to be the fire starter on a team to inspire and empower the other members of the team.

I have always looked up to others that I have learned a great deal from. Leaders like Coach Chris were positive role models and a blueprint for me on how to truly be a captain. One thing that separates him from many coaches I have come across is how controlled he is. If his team scores a point, wins a set—or even a game, for that matter—he never lets his emotions get the best of him. His postgame demeanor is always relaxed and he always refocuses his attention on the next game. At the same time, he is able to incorporate humor and fun into his coaching style. I always had this notion that being a captain meant always keeping a serious attitude on and off the court, but I could never do that with my personality. From Coach Chris I learned that being a captain also meant being yourself and learning how to use your own personality to your advantage.

One thing Shio and Armstead always stressed to us was discipline and high standards of conduct outside volleyball. Wherever we were, be it on the court or off, we had to display a high level of character in whatever it was we were doing. We needed to be a positive influence on those around us. I was lucky enough to meet people in my life who taught me the importance of what it meant to be a good person. It never occurred to me how important off-the-court things were in sports until the 2017-2018 season. Any endeavor we partake in is some extension of our life, and we need to treat whatever it is we do wholeheartedly. Part of being a captain, I realized, was being a leader and an example to others. When things were going great for us, we needed to remember to stay humble, and when things seemed hopeless (like if we were down a set), we all needed to inspire each other and raise each other's energy. I realized I had to start changing myself and how I approached everything in my life from that point on.

On Tuesday at practice after the game, everyone came in excited, and rightfully so. Shio and Armstead quickly gave us a rundown of the game by each set, and we translated whatever mistakes were most common into our drills. We started with our warm-ups and peppering and some hitting lines. Shio decided on some queen of the court, which was a miniaturized game of volleyball with three players on either side of the court. Whichever team scored a point would stay on, and the losing team would continue to rotate until the drill was finished. The drills ran smoothly, and for the most part we didn't make many mistakes.

There was one particular point during practice when I sort of had a flashback to my younger self in volleyball. I could see myself on the court, extremely nervous. There were times I should have said something to help someone out or maybe communicated more on the floor, but I always stayed quiet. After our losses the first two years, everyone would normally zone out to themselves. Our pre-game warmups were also like that. There wasn't much of a group dynamic going on, and I took responsibility for that.

So much of volleyball or any team sport really is not so much the on-the-court stuff but everything that happens off the court. It's easy to treat volleyball like a nine-to-five job and maintain disconnected relationships with teammates you may view as coworkers and leave it at that, but there is more to sports and group dynamics than that, especially in volleyball. These are people you spend a great deal of time and intimate moments with. You share in the ups and downs of a season and develop close bonds with your teammates. When you start to see a team as your own family, then how you approach the sport changes as well.

With my senior year team, I noticed we were more of a family than a team, which was why our dynamic was so special. Our off-the-floor antics were what made us so closely knitted. We took trips to Four Corners together and we all made each other laugh. It was really amazing to be a part of something like that. It wasn't always perfect. There were times when people had initial disagreements, but as time went on we actively worked to make amends and bridge our differences.

In my first year with coed, I remember not only just how poorly our season ended but how we reacted to it all. We had just finished our season with only two wins, and it took a great toll on our group dynamic. Many of us at the time, including me, were very young so we didn't really know what to do. We just thought it would be best to let Shio handle everything. In the 2015-2016 season, a similar thing happened, and again we just let time do its work, but those kinds of things can destroy a team's chemistry and identity. During the 2017-2018 season, if there were any disagreements, we actively sought to address them then and there.

Years later, I would thank Shio for making me a captain. He of course wanted me to be captain to help the team, but what he didn't realize was that it not only helped them but helped me develop into a better person. It was an honor I'll never ever forget.

It was strange that I was thinking about things like that during the year, but I guess the realization of 2018 being my last year on coed put things in perspective for me.

Chapter 19

From Watching You on the Sidelines

Our second division game was scheduled for Friday, April 13, 2018, giving us three days to rest up and readjust our strategy. We planned to give Kennedy High School a surprise. Kennedy was visiting Blair for a crucial rematch of the scrimmage game—which we won 3-0—that we had played before the season started. We knew our second go-around wouldn't be so easy. They had experience with our playing style and were hungry for revenge.

That week was a little better compared to previous ones. Our practices were a little shorter, and we didn't have the gym the whole time because of other sports needing it. Shio decided to have conditioning, given we couldn't do much volleyball-related work. One of the things we did was run the stairwell in the gym hallway, which was three stories high. At first we tried to take shortcuts by only running two flights of stairs, but Armstead and Shio caught on and stood on the top and bottom floors to make sure we were doing them fully. It was a tiresome workout and no one, even me, wanted to keep doing them. Luckily, Avery somehow convinced Shio and Armstead to abandon the conditioning and find a way to get in more volleyball practice.

The small gym was open on Wednesday, and it was the only option we had to play with a net. I hadn't been in that gym since my first-ever tryout during my sophomore year. We shared that gym with boys' varsity, giving us the ability to play against a different team and get a feel for new opponents. Coach Chris and Shio got to talking and decided to run a scrimmage game between boys and coed on Thursday before the game on Friday.

On the day of the scrimmage, I was sitting in Shio's room after school. I walked by his whiteboard, looking at the equations and work written on them. I noticed Brenna's name on the left end of the whiteboard. On it she had written, "Dear Math, I'm sorry I don't understand you. It's not me, it's you. It's over." I nearly fell to the ground laughing. I sent it to our group chat and the reactions I got made me laugh even more.

The team met outside the small gym. I'm not sure how other coed and boys' teams in the county treated each other, but there was always a little rivalry between us at Blair. There were always debates about who was a better player or who could beat other teams if they had the chance. In my first two years, it was clear coed had no shot against the boys team, but the 2018 year was different. We scrimmaged them with no limitations on substitutions, which allowed everyone to play. Like a real game, Coach Chris stood on his side with his players while Shio with Armstead were on the other side. To allow a mix of rotations and lineups, coed moved pieces around to force everyone to learn how to adapt to new players they had not played with much.

At first the boys got an early lead and were dominating us at the net. It took time for us to adapt to their playing style and their unique player tendencies. Eventually, we fought back to tie the game. With every rotation, we took some time to adjust and we lost points, but we would always come back. Toward the end, Shio put the starting lineup in and it was lights out after that. What started out as a friendly match ended up taking on the intensity of a real game. We all were diving for balls and yelling out different calls, and our play reflected a playoff atmosphere. At one point I even dove for a ball and ended up landing awkwardly, bruising myself. It hadn't been necessary, but we wanted to drive the point that coed was no longer the little brother to boys. Needless to say, there were no more arguments about who was better from that day on.

At home I checked my phone to see if there were any serious conversations happening in our group chat. Of course the topic of debate was spirit wear again. Brenna wanted pajama day. Olivia wanted red out. It was predicted to be over 80 degrees, so pajamas maybe were a good idea. With my captain card, I changed it to spring wear. "Lmaoooooo," Noah texted in response. I told everyone to hydrate and stay ready for tomorrow.

Finally, it was Friday, April 13, 2018, the day of the Kennedy game. We set up the nets and began warming up. "God's Plan" came over the speaker system. Players from Kennedy began trickling into our gym until there was a sea of green. Their setter was a very tall boy, which was unusual to see in coed. Usually, teams had a girl setter to guarantee a girl would touch a ball at least once. Coed rules state that a girl must touch the ball at least once before it goes over the net, apart from some exceptions. With their setter being a boy, we knew we could use that to our advantage.

Captains were called and Fiona and I won the coin toss again. We elected to serve.

The game started out with a great deal of intensity. We could tell Kennedy had done their homework and had made adjustments based on their last game with us. We had also improved since our last meeting and had a few new tricks up our sleeves. Noah and Brenna controlled the net. Fiona's setting was spectacular. Olivia and I were handling it on the offensive side, and Tyler, along with

Tiffany and Avery, were unstoppable on defense. We slowly took over the game and dominated the first two sets.

For the third set Shio decided to let other players get game time experience. We had a nice comfortable lead, and it would be a good opportunity for the younger players to better understand the atmosphere and clear up any confusion about rotations or schematics.

For the last set, Shio kept Tyler, Fiona, and Brenna in. He subbed in River, Mizan, and Ruben. They were all underclassmen but very talented. Mizan was the only left-handed player at Blair and had the most consistent hitting form of anyone on the team. River was extremely energetic and, in a span of weeks, had learned and excelled at every aspect of volleyball. River's positive energy was always a source of inspiration and excitement for us. Ruben played soccer outside school, giving him an athletic advantage over others. He had even earned Blair a couple of aces throughout the year. His reaction time and serving were really good that day. Tyler finished the game out with an ace from a jump serve to secure another 3-0 win.

We packed our things and headed home. In our group chat everyone poured out their excitement. Jaya congratulated us on our "a** kicking skills." Tyler and Olivia used the word "thrash," which I had never heard before, but it was catching on in coed. I told them all to rest up for Saturday practice and stay well rested for the upcoming week. Three games were scheduled— Monday, Wednesday, and Friday—which meant we had to make sure we dieted properly and kept a good schedule to get enough rest throughout the week. Our next three games would close out our division season.

Saturday practice had a little better turnout than usual. We were inspired to come because we wanted to get better at volleyball, or at least that's what we told Coach Armstead as she was passing out donuts to everyone. Toward the end of our session, we just sat around and talked. I remember being so tired that I assumed the next day was Monday and asked what time our game was in the group chat. Everyone freaked out, thinking there was a game on Sunday. We had random conversations about anything and everything. Elisabeth brought up bruised knees, a topic many of our players were all too familiar with. Tyler, who was known to get hurt a lot because of constant diving during games and practices, suggested they weren't that bad and, in true Tyler fashion, encouraged everyone to not wear knee pads. Tiffany said she couldn't remember the last time her knees were not bruised. We went on for hours before calling it a night.

On Monday, April 16, 2018, we waited for the bus to take us to Wheaton High School for our third division game. Jaya, who had returned, was driving there on her own and asked if anyone could let her know when the bus left Blair. Noah responded with a simple, "No," to which she responded "Thanks, Noah, ." Those little antics of ours kept the mood relaxed. We could always look to each other for comfort when we needed to control our worries before a game.

Wheaton had remodeled their buildings a couple of years prior. Their volleyball gym was probably one of the more beautiful ones in the entire county. We walked in for the first time and were amazed by how colorful and new everything looked, and better yet, they had a high ceiling! The only thing that was a little worrisome was a divider on the ceiling parallel to the net, which meant we had to watch how high we passed the ball over in case a play broke down.

We warmed up as usual, and captains were called. Jaya was back, so we both went for the coin toss. It felt weird after not having her for the last three games. She was our floor general and her absence had really been felt. As always I told her what to pick, and we won the coin toss again. We elected to serve.

A couple of years prior, we lost a game against Wheaton on their home court. We were the clear-cut better team that year, but our overconfidence gave them the upset. Shio knew the same thing could happen again. He called us in for a huddle and took us back to that game. "Remember what happened here last time. We thought we were going to win and ended up losing. Let's not have that happen again. Remember, always communicate and trust each other. Let's get a Blair on three." We broke the huddle and went back to our original lineup.

We served a couple of aces to start the match. Wheaton responded but our overall team play was much better than theirs. For the most part we controlled the sets. They made it a fight in the third set, but we edged out a victory with a 3-0 win. I looked over at the bleachers and saw Tyler's dad again. As always, he was one of the few people who came to all our games, especially the away ones.

With the win against Wheaton, Blair was on a four-game winning streak, putting our overall record at 5-1, the only loss coming from Sherwood.

Shaking hands with Wheaton players after our win.

We were scheduled to play Northwood, our school rivals, on Wednesday, April 18, just two days away. Because that week was a three-game week, practice would be held only twice—on Tuesday and Thursday—but we could not fully maximize our time because of injury risks. Those were some of the hardest weeks during the season, given there was not much time to rest or fully enjoy our wins.

To add even more to our busy schedule, I saw the words "pep rally" in a notification on my phone. *Oh my god,* I thought, *I completely forgot about the pep rally.* The spring pep rally was scheduled for Friday that same week, the same day as our final division game. River asked if something was happening with sports walk-outs. The previous year, Blair had decided to not have teams run out and be introduced as usual. For the 2018 year, they had gone back to the old format.

The rivalry between Blair and Northwood was dubbed "the Battle of the Boulevard" because both schools are located on University Boulevard, which is the most recognizable and famous street in the area. Northwood at the time wasn't a very good team, but we still needed to take that game seriously, given the rivalry. It would also be a good morale boost for our final division game.

Northwood was an extremely close drive from Blair, which meant we had to prepare a little earlier than usual due to how early they would arrive. Underclassmen pulled the floor. Miles, who was on the team at the beginning of the season, didn't show for the game. Apparently, he had left for some reason and wouldn't return. That was a little blow for the future of Blair volleyball.

Northwood arrived early wearing their dark black uniforms. They looked fired up and ready to pull off an upset, but we weren't going to let that happen. We warmed up to "God's Plan" and won the coin toss, just like I told Jaya we would. You'd think after winning it every game she would trust me with the coin toss thing, but she still was a little hesitant.

The Northwood game was one of our smoother ones that season. We didn't have any problems for the most part and controlled the floor all the way through for a clean 3-0 sweep of our rivals. That win felt really good for me personally. It was nice to win at home after they had come to Blair two years prior and beaten us in front of a big home crowd. The Northwood win put our overall record at 6-1, with a 4-0 division record. We had one game to go to win the division.

As we were packing our things and heading out, Shio came over to me with a very big smile on his face. I knew something was up but I couldn't decipher what it was. "Great job today," he said.

"Thanks." Usually, he never let his emotions show, but I knew how much a division title meant to him. We both happened to be standing right under the coed banner. I looked up and found myself fixated on its emptiness. I knew what it would mean, not only to me but to everyone, just to see the number "2018" painted across that banner.

Our next game was not going to be easy, but laid out in front of us was the opportunity to finally accomplish what no Blair coed volleyball team ever had.

Shio gave me a high five and we called it a night.

Chapter 20

Dreaming of Victory

Usually, in volleyball, teams have a single setter for the entire season and a backup in case of an injury. With our senior team, Shio wanted to utilize the plethora of talent we had, especially at the setter position. In volleyball, setting is a really prestigious and sacred position. The setter is not only the captain on the court and extension of the coaches, but everything that happens on the court happens through the setter. With volleyball in particular, over the course of a game, opposing teams get to fully analyze the playing style of any setter. They learn about their tendencies, strengths, and weaknesses.

Jaya had joined the coed team during the 2016-2017 season. Over the course of games, we noticed teams adjusting to how we played, and because any volleyball team is centered around their setter, teams ultimately adjust to the opposing team as a whole. When a team adjusts, there is little you can change, given that you've practiced with one person doing similar things over and over again. That changed during the 2017-2018 season when Fiona joined.

We developed a sort of one-two punch with setting. Fiona was extremely talented, so having them sit out an entire season would have been a waste. We instituted a new system at Blair to run a double-setter offense. During practice, the starters alternated with each setter, as it was crucial for hitters to develop chemistry with both setters. Of course the fundamentals were important, like how to approach a hit or correct ball placement when setting, but only through practice can you really find that sweet spot where the connection between hitter and setter becomes graceful and automatic.

Jaya and I, as well as other players like Olivia and Brenna, had already developed chemistry, given our previous year playing together. The newcomers, as well as the addition of Fiona, meant we had to learn and adjust to Fiona's style of setting. It was a learning experience for us hitters and one that we needed crucially because it expanded our talent. Because Jaya and Fiona had two different play styles, we could simultaneously refine our skills while also learning new team dynamics. It was a profound experience, and the results of our experiences really showed on the court.

Jaya and Fiona also added two new dimensions to our team, not just from a volleyball standpoint but also in terms of their personalities and execution on the floor. Jaya was not as energetic as Fiona; she was more what I like to call a silent assassin. She did not yell too loudly or show her emotions, but behind it all she was deadly with setting. During games, she'd go over to anyone who needed help and quietly whisper words of encouragement. Her serving was also a reflection of who she was. Her approach was slow and elegant, yet as she made contact with the ball, its randomized movement made it hard for defenses to receive it.

Fiona was the exact opposite. They were more of a high-energy player. They were loud on the court, and their willpower far exceeded any of ours. There was no pass Fiona wouldn't go for. At times our passes were so bad that they had to run across the entire floor, and still, somehow, Fiona managed to set a perfect ball for a kill. As a team, learning those new styles and finding a balance between them really changed our play for the better.

Shio and Armstead rotated between Jaya and Fiona during games to put other teams off guard. As a defense, you almost have to change your entire scheme, because your strategy is only applicable for one single setter. Throwing in another setter creates new offensive dynamics that you have to account for. The fun didn't stop there. Shio rotated between Jaya and Fiona over and over again, continuously throwing the opposing team off balance as they attempted to adjust multiple times during a game, and before they knew it, the set was over. It was a really cool and unique aspect of our team that year.

We didn't know it at the time, but Fiona joining the team would also be a saving grace for us. Jaya missed three games early on, and had Fiona not been there, we may not have won those games. Anyone who knows the sport of volleyball knows that setting is not just the hardest position in volleyball but one of the hardest positions in any sport. It really is a holistic position. Just as the quarterback of a football team is the centerpiece, as is the point guard in basketball, or even the central player in soccer, the setter is everything. What makes it such a hard position is that the setter has to understand what the opponent gives them from a defensive standpoint and how to react to it. They also have to then decide which player to set and what kind of set to give, all in a matter of seconds.

I really didn't understand how hard setting was until one week when Shio decided to try something different. Shio wanted a boy to run setting to see how things went during the week. It was a little into the season, and we were experimenting with different playstyles to somehow add to our system at Blair. Avery, Tyler, and I were the candidates chosen. I can tell you right now that I was—and still am—a terrible setter. It was never something I was perfect at, and I was not on the level of Tyler and Avery. Tyler was too important to remove on defense, so Avery was chosen to set. With his all-around skills, should a play ever break down, he had the means to improvise better than any of us.

We ran a couple of initial plays but kept forgetting about the coed rule regarding a girl having to touch the ball at least once before it went over the net. Shio or Armstead would simulate a hit or serve over, sometimes even a free ball, which we preferred. Tyler would receive it and pass it to Avery, who would then set it to me, and while it was happening, everyone would yell, "Girl, girl, girl!"

I remember a very funny incident when Shio simulated a tip that I dug up. Avery set it to Tyler, and as he was going to hit the ball, he realized no girl had touched it, so he just froze mid-air and fell to the ground, along with the ball. We all dropped, laughing so hard that it was hard to breathe for a few minutes.

The Avery-led team even got game time for a whole set against our weaker opponents. It was difficult to adjust to, but we managed it. The experience was a nice way to be more appreciative and thankful for our wonderful setters Jaya and Fiona. There were times when we had to constantly yell, "Girl, girl, girl!" during games to remind ourselves of the coed rule. Other times, because we didn't have much time to mesh together, Avery would set a perfect ball but the hitters would be very far off with their timing.

We tried to add new concepts to our team to switch up hitting and setting. Shio knew as we inched toward the playoffs that teams were only going to get better, so we had to add more dimensions to our already existing toolkit of volleyball tricks. The first thing we added—or attempted to add—was the fast tempo set. On a normal set, the hitter has time to approach and a setter sets the ball high, giving lots of air time. With a quick set, this was all sped up using a lower and quicker ball. The approach had to be timed just right to come a bit early so that as you jumped and swung, the ball met your hands at the net with a lower and faster trajectory. I tried it with Jaya but we failed quite a lot. It took a very long time before we could get the timing right, but even then it was only in a trial phase.

The hitters all rotated with Jaya and Fiona, learning new hitting techniques and plays. For our middle, we had a back set, which was essentially a play where the middle hitter would approach but go behind the setter. Normally, players run in front of a setter, but this was a way of throwing opposing defenders off. It was both fast and unexpected. Brenna was much more efficient than Noah, given her experience with Jaya and middle hitting.

For the right side, we worked on fake calls, which were a fake set to either the outside or middle and an actual set behind the setter to the right side. Of course there was no way to fake the hit, because the right-side hitter had to know whether or not they were being set, so we came up with a code of sorts. On normal plays, the hitters would call out their position and be set in said position, but if the setter called something, then that meant a fake was coming and the right-side hitter had to be ready to go. This went back to Shio stressing our communication. That was at the heart of our team.

Setters were not just floor generals but also people you could confide in when you needed advice on anything. Jaya and Fiona were like the glue that held us together. If anyone needed advice on anything, like school, work, relationships, or volleyball, they always welcomed them with open arms. I remember during my second year with coed that, after many of my losses, Jaya and I often talked for extended periods of time, and somehow, through all the defeats, we found a way to smile and look forward. Even during the 2017-2018 season, there were some rough times, especially with the political climate and the fears students had for their lives after events like the shootings in Florida. Jaya and Fiona, the inspirational and comforting leaders, took everyone under their wings and really transcended beyond their setter positions.

Those little details are what you remember most about a team and people as time passes. Sometimes, I forget how lucky I was to be surrounded by those amazing people, and it is only when I look back that I can really understand how special our team was.

Chapter 21

To Holding Up a Trophy of a Lifetime

Thursday, after the Northwood game, emotions were at an all-time high. It was the day before arguably the biggest game in coed volleyball history at Blair, so everyone was on high alert. In our group chat, we went back and forth about pregame warmup songs. Of course, I suggested "God's Plan." Olivia suggested listening to the Walmart yodeling kid. We all assumed the starting time for the game was either 5:30 or after 7:00 like all other games, but for some reason this game was scheduled for 3:45, just an hour and 15 minutes after school ended. Jaya split the spiritwear between upper- and underclassmen: red for upper and white for lower.

The pep rally was usually not very interesting for coed volleyball, but for 2018 it was much different. Shio had ordered custom-made under-armor quarter-zips for us, which were really cool. It was nice to finally have some team spirit to represent volleyball, and it went perfectly with the whole pep rally vibe.

After school on Thursday, my cousin and I were in Shio's room, like we were every other day. Shio was usually out grading papers or something, but this time he happened to come in a little early. I could see the excitement on his face. He had a very contagious smile.

We all expected practice to be brutal that day, but it ended up being the most fun practice all year long. Shio later told me that he had wanted everyone to be relaxed and not have to worry about winning or losing but to have the chance to just enjoy playing volleyball and goof around in practice. It was because of his decision to change up practice that day that everyone was very relaxed and ready for our final division game.

Friday's game was against Rockville High School, which had won the division the previous three years. With the game scheduled earlier than usual, it was a tight squeeze to get in a practice because of the pep rally that same day. We all went over last-minute things like what time to arrive and when to set up the gym. Shio and Armstead asked us to let our friends know about the game to get a nice crowd, given the circumstances. Ms. Boule also made announcements and advertised the game for us, which was nice because we never really had a packed home crowd.

I woke up Friday morning, April 20, 2018, and proceeded with my usual morning routine. It still hadn't hit me how big that day was as I drove to school with the windows down and my music playing. The bright red of my new quarter-zip really gave me a sense of confidence and comfort that I needed.

I walked through the back entrance of the school where the cafeteria was and strolled down Blair Boulevard to my morning art class. I glanced at some of my teammates who happened to be sitting along the boulevard. We didn't say anything to each other, just nodded. I entered my classroom and maneuvered my way through the sea of desks to the back. As I passed one of my classmates, he turned to me and said, "Oh, you're on coed volleyball, right?"

I nodded.

"Yeah, I'm coming to your game along with some friends," he said.

I was pleasantly surprised. Those announcements were actually getting people's attention. That morning they aired InfoFlow with an announcement about our upcoming division game. I was so excited that I texted everyone: **"We on Infoflow!!!!"** Coed was never really on Infoflow, so you can imagine the excitement of seeing yourself on screen.

I went about my day as usual until my final period, which was when all athletes were called to leave class early and line up with their respective sports for the spring pep rally runout. I took the stairwell down and exited from the back of the school to the practice field just outside the turf field. There were hundreds of students scattered around. It was a giant sea of red. I floated about until I saw the coed team at a distance. We all gathered together and talked about nothing else except the division championship game. Everyone was worried about not having enough time to set up and warm up because the pep rally could go on longer than intended.

As the sounds of hundreds of students began to fade away, I had a moment to myself when I looked around at everything happening. It hit me then how special that day was. Not so much the volleyball part only but the fact that it was my last year in high school. Time had gone by so quickly. It seemed only yesterday that I was a freshman, and here I was, a senior about to partake in one final pep rally. I asked if everyone wanted to do a team picture to sort of celebrate our time together and our final pep rally. Taking it after the game would ruin the whole picture thing if we lost, so we agreed to do it after the pep rally. It would give us something to enjoy just in case we were to lose the game.

We waited patiently for our names to be called. One after another, different sports ran out to the sound of cheers from over 3,000 students. Jaya and I lined up in the front with our red quarter-zips. She held a sign in her hand with the words "Varsity Coed Volleyball" written on it. Behind us were Noah, Isabelle, Olivia, Edward, Ruben, Elisabeth, River, Mizan, Abby, and Fiona. Just before our names were called, I decided to pull my phone out and selfie record our walk together. It just felt like a good time to document that moment, and I am glad I did.

Coed walking out during the spring pep rally.

A fellow classmate with a microphone called us out and announced our upcoming game with a division title on the line. As he said those words, the crowd erupted in cheers. It sent shivers down my spine when I heard that thunderous sound. It was a slow walk, but every second of it was a reminder of our journey to where we had ended up.

The pep rally went on for about an hour, and as we fumbled our way through the hordes of students to find each other, we realized there wasn't enough time for a picture. We all sprinted to the main gym to set up and get ready for the game.

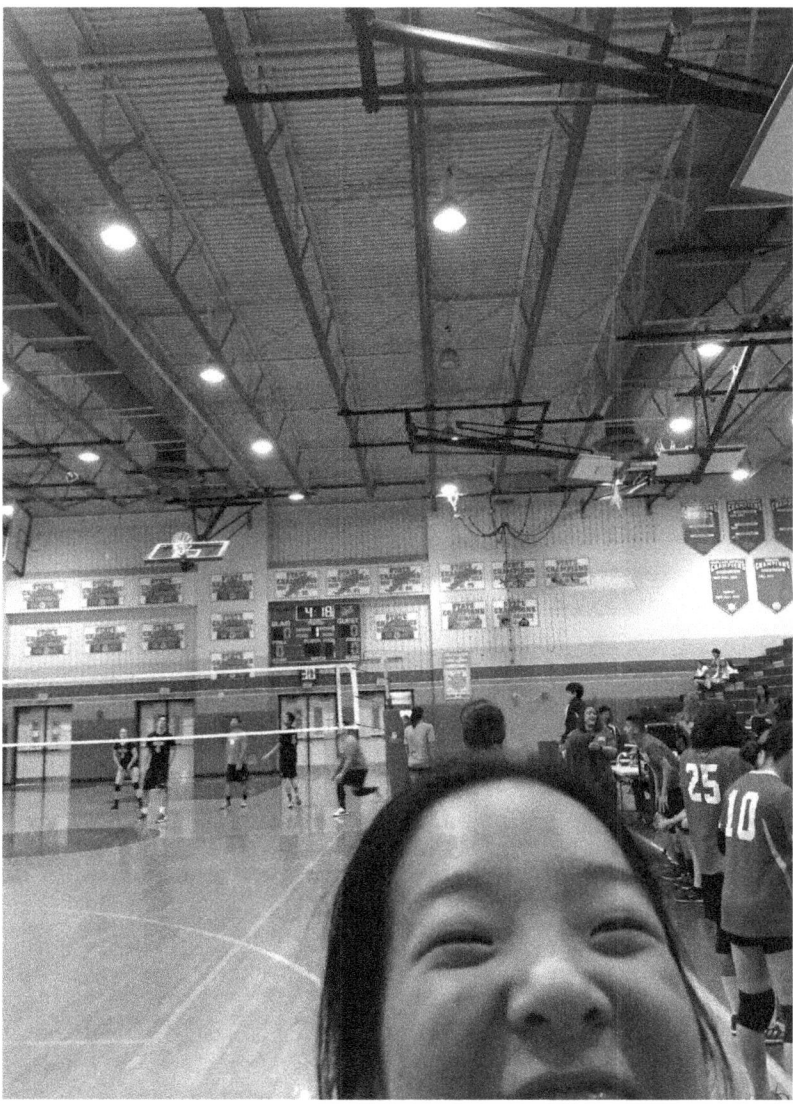

Ariel with a photobomb before the coed divisional championship game against Rockville.

As we were setting up the nets and chairs, we watched as families slowly began pouring into the gym. At first it was like any other home game, with only a handful of parents and some students coming to watch their friends. But that day, as time went on, it was spectacular to see how many people turned up. Groups of people entered the main gym in anticipation of our game. The intensity was starting to heat up. As I grabbed a ball to go practice my hitting, I yelled across the court to Ms. Boule, "That's a lot of people."

She turned to me, and with no hesitation, responded, "We're winning that trophy today."

I turned away and went to practice, with my smile now widened more than before.

Hitters were against the wall away from the bleachers, warming up. Initially, we turned the music off to allow everyone to get into their own zones. I had my headphones on as I practiced my arm swings. To my left were other hitters, like Olivia, Noah, and Brenna. To my back, Tyler, Avery, and Tiffany were working on a three-person passing drill. I noticed everyone's heads turn toward the entrance of the gym.

Rockville had arrived. They wore dark black uniforms. It was an all-too-familiar sight. They beat us in clean 3-0 sweeps both away and at home in previous years. Shio turned our

Blair Coed Volleyball watching Rockville during their warmup.

attention away from them and told us to get back to practicing.

The buzzer rang and the start of pregame warmups was officially underway. Captains were called. I was standing next to Jaya when Shio joined us some seconds later, wearing his red Blair polo and black shorts. He seemed calm. Jaya and I were beyond excited. We couldn't contain our energy. As the ref went over the rules and coin toss, I leaned over to Jaya and whispered, "Watch, we're going to win the coin toss." She seemed a bit confused but we won again!

"Serve," said Shio when asked by the ref what his team wanted to do.

Shio and Armstead called us over for a huddle. They brought our attention to the empty banner for coed volleyball. "You guys see that over there. You have a chance right now to change that. But I don't want you to think about that right now. Right now I just want you to play volleyball. The score is always nothing to nothing," said Armstead. Shio stressed fundamentals and communication like he always did.

The lineup for that game started out with Jaya, Tyler, Avery, Tiffany, Brenna, and me. The six of us watched as Rockville chose their starting lineup. "We got this," said Tyler.

We served the ball over. Rockville received and set it to the outside.

"Outside! Outside!" I yelled as the six of us transitioned for an outside attack. Our backcourt received their hit and I was set. I approached and swung hard, sending the ball flying down the middle just in front of Rockville's middle back position for an easy kill. We all yelled and cheered. A couple more points and we were on a roll.

The Rockville setter hit us with a dump. It was unexpected but, at the same time, common for them to do. Just the previous year, on this very day, we had traveled to Rockville and lost 3-0. The majority of the points Rockville had scored that day were because of our own mistakes as a result of not being ready on defense. The setter dump was one of the plays that had hurt us the most.

Now we huddled together and Avery yelled, "My bad. I'll get that next time." Jaya instructed us to watch for more of those as the game went on, especially when we least expected it. We adjusted our defense a little to take away obvious spots for dumps, which left the back two corners a little more exposed. But with Tyler and Tiffany on defense, it wasn't much of a problem.

Rockville was having a hard time hitting on offense with our height at the net on the part of Brenna and Noah. Olivia, Noah, and I were handling business on offense. We won the first set to go up 1-0.

As we switched sides, we glanced over at the scoreboard just on top of the exit door. "No one looks at the scoreboard," said Shio. He wanted to keep our attention on the game. In volleyball, each set is in itself a miniature game. If a set ends, that "game" has now ended, so you look to the next. Armstead pulled out her clipboard and showed us her stats for the set. For the most part we had been in control, but there were some minor defensive mistakes we could correct. Serving was going well and hitting was off the charts. Our priority was to keep our mental focus in check.

Rockville served over to begin the second set. Their serves weren't easy to receive but we slowly adjusted to them. The second set was not much different than the first. We controlled both sides of the game and took a 2-0 lead.

Shio was getting more nervous. Having played with him for two years, we had been a part of both comebacks from being 2-0 down and losses when we had a 2-0 lead. In volleyball, momentum is such an important thing, as it is in any sport. All it takes is for the winning team to relax for just a bit and light a spark on the opponent's side. If momentum swings, then chances of an upset vastly increase.

I called everyone to a mini huddle. This wasn't about a 3-0 win; we had to play as if it was the first set all over again. I know from previous experience that it was very easy to look at the scoreboard over and over again and get lost in the numbers. You start to worry so much about each point that it can cause you to spiral down, so I told everyone to forget the fact that we were up two sets. "Think of this as the first set. We're not playing to twenty-five points. We're just playing to one point. If you make a mistake, shake it off and worry about the next point."

Rockville was putting up a very good fight. They started to get louder and gain more momentum, but we quickly took care of the fire early on with blocks from Noah and Brenna. Toward the end of the set, I looked up at the scoreboard and noticed we had five points left to score to win the game. I was standing across from Jaya just as we were about to transition for defense before the serve. "Can you believe we're about to win division for the first time ever?" I whispered to her.

"Let's finish this quick," she said, an exhausted look on her face.

Our emotions were slowly starting to show. With every point the cheers became louder and the bleachers became more thunderous.

For the final point, Rockville served over. I was standing in the right-side position behind Jaya. Back to receive were Tyler, Elisabeth, and Avery. The pass flew over the net directly in front of Tyler. He shuffled up with ease and passed to Jaya.

"Outside, outside!" yelled Avery as she set the ball to him.

I watched as the ball slowly drifted downward. Avery approached and with a lightning strike sent the ball over the net. One of the Rockville players tried to receive it, but it shanked off their arm and flew to the back of the court. The whole gym erupted in cheers. Everyone on the sidelines jumped and screamed. I immediately turned around and went to Shio, giving him the biggest hug ever. "We did it," I yelled in his ears.

"Nice job. Now it's on to county," he responded.

The cheers lasted for a long time. Ms. Boule, along with all the parents and our friends from school, came down to congratulate us. We all shook hands with the Rockville players and ran to our end of the floor. We gathered to take a picture and celebrate three years' worth of waiting.

I can't explain the feeling that day. I had dreamed of that moment since my first year on coed and there I was, actually living it. Everyone joined in for the photo. We posed for many photos, making silly faces, throwing up our hands, and beaming with smiles. I had a moment to myself when I looked out onto the court and breathed a sigh of relief. So much hard work had gone into this—and it was worth every bit.

We took down the nets, celebrating various moments from the game as we paced between the gym and the equipment room. Everyone was smiling and there was a sense of pure joy in the air. We packed our things and headed out to the student parking lot in front of the school. The cheers continued all the way home. My cousin and I were heading home together. As we sat in the car, we let go of ourselves for a minute. "We actually did it," I said to him.

"Aziz, quickly, let's go home, we have to pray," he said.

Team photo after winning the division!

I arrived home that day with the biggest smile on my face. Opening the door, I was greeted by my uncle, who asked why we were so happy.

"Nothing," I said. "Just a very good day."

I showered and changed, with every second a reminder of moments flashing in and out of my head. I pictured plays happening and the cheers along with it. My phone was screaming with notifications from all over. One by one I opened them all. Twitter was first.

Our win was all over Twitter. The Blair Sports Twitter page, along with Mrs. Johnson, Blazer Ragers, and Tyler's dad, posted our group photo and final play. As I continued to scroll, my smile grew wider.

Division Champions!!" wrote Blair Sports.

"Match point. That's what division championship tastes like!" wrote Mr. Fong.

"HUGE SHOUTOUT TO BLAIR VOLLEYBALL! BLAZERS VOLLEYBALL WON DIVISIONS FOR THE FIRST TIME IN BLAIR HISTORY" wrote Mrs. Johnson and the Blair Sports page.

The congratulations continued to pour in. Our photo was all over Twitter as well. The highlight definitely was Noah to the left of the screen, holding his hand down and forming a zero with his index finger and thumb. It was the gesture that was invented in which a person holds their hand below their waist, forming a circle with their index and thumb. If anyone looks into the circle, they "got your neck."

Our group chat was buzzing with notifications as well. River sent the first message in all capital letters—"DIVISION CHAMPS"—followed by "Yeah!" from multiple people and congratulations from various team members. I scrolled down more until I saw a message from Noah asking, "So is next for the county?"

I froze when I saw that question. It seemed to make me forget about the division win. That was now something behind me, and my eyes were set on something else: winning county. With the way our team was playing that year, I knew we had a legitimate shot at winning county, which would also be the first time in school history. Our overall record was 7-1, putting us in the top three in the county rankings.

Before I spiraled down into a whole new world of looking onward, I decided to call it a night and enjoy winning our division.

Chapter 22

Making History

Over the course of a season, there are often miraculous or strange things that happen that add a sense of magic to the experience of playing sports. During my last year with coed, I decided to try to create some magic at Blair. One thing I always found particularly intriguing was the pregame coin toss. On the surface, its primary purpose was to give the winner of the coin toss the choice to either serve or receive. Beneath the surface, however, there was more to it than that. The advantage of having the choice to control the way you start can affect the outcome of an entire volleyball game. It could be the difference between gaining momentum and losing it. The fun part about it, though, was that there was no real cost if you made the wrong choice because, ultimately, it was out of one's hands.

Although it was impossible to predict how the coin toss would go, I thought it would be fun to see if I could maybe get the volleyball magic on our side for that 2018 season. I informed Jaya before every game that Blair was going to win the coin toss. I never said anything more. I walked up to her before each home game and said, "We're winning the coin toss. Do you want to serve or receive?" She always gave me a look of immense confusion. For away games, I told her which side of the coin to pick. It worked every time. We won every coin toss that entire season, wherever I performed my pregame ritual.

Shio asked us about it one day, but I didn't want to break the spell, so I just told him to trust me and go along with our little ritual. The best part about it was telling everyone on the team later on. People kept wondering why we always served first, so I told them. I wish you could have been there to see their reactions. That kind of magic was absent my first two years with coed.

As the season neared its end, I would often reflect on weird and unique things, like the coin toss phenomenon. Funny enough, I realized it was much like how the season had gone. Just like our coin toss, wins were unexpected, and so was our season, but at the same time, something about it felt almost miraculous. The pregame coin toss was something I would come to miss dearly years later. Although it was something very minute, knowing a game would follow made it more than a coin toss. It's the little things you do regularly in life but fail to notice that you miss most later on. Things aligned in the universe in just the right way that season to give us unforgettable moments of wonder, even with something as simple as a coin toss.

Chapter 23

I Never Wanted It to End

Saturday practice was scheduled again right after our division win. We had another upcoming week with multiple games, which meant we had to quickly enjoy our win and then refocus on the next game.

"DIVISION CHAMPS," River texted again.

I knew that was something that would occupy our minds for the rest of the season, but as Shio told me after our win, we needed to move on and look toward achieving bigger goals. Saturday morning before practice we created a Snapchat group to host debates about the silliest of topics. We argued about whether or not water was wet, what the greatest show of all time was (it's obviously "Friends!") or whether cats or dogs were a better choice for a pet. Olivia asked everyone to drop their usernames.

I was the first to send a message to our new group chat: "**Goals for this year: go 10-1 Win counties.**"

"**Extensive,**" Avery responded.

It may have been extensive, but constantly looking back at our division win would not do anything to help us move forward We needed a new goal to chase, but at that point in time, the most important task at hand was preparing for the upcoming game that week on Monday against Wootton High School.

Practice went surprisingly well, and the division win had a great deal to do with that. We had gained much-needed confidence and had a great number of games under our belt, aiding in team chemistry and giving us enough stats to analyze our strengths and weaknesses. For the most part we stuck to simple and easy drills to let our bodies rest a little.

Sunday night I got a text from Noah saying he might not be able to make it to Monday's game due to an illness. That made everyone worry because, without a middle, much of our rotations without Brenna would be exposed to offensive attacks, putting more stress on our backrow. With three games to go in the season, each game mattered greatly for the overall county rankings. The higher seeds would have a home-court advantage in the playoffs. With our top four ranking, all our playoff games would be at home unless we were to meet a team ranked above us, which was only possible toward the later rounds of playoffs.

The top four teams in the county at the time were Sherwood, Churchill, Clarksburg, and Blair. One thing working in our favor was that two of the top four teams were playing the upcoming Monday, giving us a chance to inch up another spot. We started to delve deeply into all the possible outcomes that could affect our ranking. Thankfully, Jaya stepped in and reminded everyone of the priorities at hand, helping us refocus our attention on more pressing matters.

On Monday, April 23, 2018, we were scheduled to play an away game at Wootton High School. I woke up extremely excited that day, not just because of our game but also because that same week Marvel's long-awaited *Avengers: Infinity War* movie was being released in theatres. I was—and still am—a massive comic book superhero fan, and the momentous event had been 10 years in the making. I texted everyone in the chat about the movie, and of course Jaya and I had our DC vs Marvel teasing. It sparked a group debate about comics and superheroes that continued all the way until we left for Wootton.

Wootton was an all too familiar experience I had to relive many times. They had one of the most hostile environments in the entire county because of how passionate their fans were. Of all the schools in the county, they had a consistent crowd turnout for volleyball games, making our games there that much tougher.

We walked into Wootton and, like always, got lost trying to find the gym, which was on the upper floor of the school. As we entered, their players had already set up the nets, and the bleachers had a good amount of people already waiting for the game to begin. Our side of the bleachers was much less packed. But Mr. Fong, as always, was there to cheer us on.

I got changed and sat at the top of the bleachers near my cousin. We talked for a little while, reminiscing about our first time in the Wootton gym. I remember watching Wootton's warmups and thinking that it wasn't going to be an easy game. They had a very strong team, and from what the girls varsity players told us, they were not to be taken lightly. They had all-around players in every position, so not only was their core team strong, but they had depth on their roster.

We warmed up outside the gym, running laps in the hallways and doing some dynamic stretching. As we maneuvered our way through the seemingly never-ending turns, we went over game plans and individual assignments. Noah was not there, so blocking was prioritized to take away the direct kill spots for their outside hitters and to close the middle attack. Wootton was returning some coed players from the previous year, so we had to adjust some things because they had hitters all around who were now more experienced against our team. Warmups began in the gym with both teams practicing on either side of the court. Captains were called and as always, I whispered to Jaya what side of the coin to pick. We won it again!

Blair served first. With Noah out, the lineup had to be switched a little. There would be fewer substitutions, and Tyler would stay in for all rotations, giving him some opportunities to hit at the net and block.

The first set started with Wotton rallying off some points. Having no tall middle blocker was hurting us immensely. Wootton was getting free open kills, and our defense had way too many holes, leaving us vulnerable. Our offense was doing great, but with the defense doing poorly, we couldn't pull away with a lead. It was always a fight from behind. During the last points of the first set, on one particular play I was playing middle back. I watched the ball get set to the outside and hit directly at me. It looked like it was going out, but it dipped at the last second, hitting the end line and giving Wootton the final point to win the set.

I looked over at Coach Chris, who happened to be sitting near our sidelines. Using his hands, he signaled a minor tweak on defense. He was asking me to change my base defense position. That was our first time losing an opening set since the Einstein game.

Our nerves were starting to slowly creep in. Not having a middle was really hurting our rotation, and it was disrupting our usual playing style. Shio decided to make some changes, in particular how we set up blocking. Rather than having one blocker attempt to stop the middle attacks, we would institute either two- or three-person blocks. For middle attacks, he instructed the two outside hitters to close in on Wootton's middle blockers, essentially forming a wall that would take away their opportunities for open hits. As always, communication was essential. We had lost our communication toward the end of the first set a little, so we prioritized getting that back.

The second set started the same way as the first. This time we gathered ourselves and focused on earning one point at a time. From then on, we picked up the pace, and slowly but surely, our defense stopped Wootton's attack. We gradually pulled away with a lead and closed out the second set to tie it at 1-1.

The next two sets were competitive battles, but our adjustments on defense ultimately outplayed Wootton, leading to a 3-1 comeback win from behind. It was a great win and we all cheered. Shio and Armstead called us over to congratulate us. That was our first win of the year under such difficult circumstances. It was similar to losing Jaya for those three games early in the year, but this time we'd had a setter who could fill her shoes.

Shaking hands with each other after our win against Wootton.

In the case of the Wootton game, we had no other boy player with Noah's height, but our adjustments were what gave us that crucial win. That game also added another dimension to our team, one we were glad to have as we inched our way to the end of the season with playoffs approaching. Knowing we could win under such circumstances as not having a pivotal piece to our team was a great confidence boost but also a stark reminder about how we needed everyone to be on the court if we were to truly actualize our talents.

I arrived home with more congratulatory messages flooding my phone. Noah was informed of the win, but more importantly, the county rankings had changed. Sherwood had beaten Churchill, which meant that three of the top four ranked teams had one loss each. With our loss at Sherwood, we were ranked below them, but because we hadn't played Churchill, the deciding factor for the third spot came down to which team had won more sets in the year thus far.

With Churchill having won more sets, we were given the number-four spot, with Sherwood at two, undefeated Clarksburg at one, and Churchill at three. Tyler said that Clarksburg was to play Churchill soon, which could have more impact on the rankings. It might give us the number-three spot, but that was out of our control. All we could do was focus on winning the rest of our games and then worry about the playoff seeding. Our conversations continued late into the night, but with another game just two days away, we finally called it a night.

—◊—

At practice on Tuesday, we worked on adjustment plays similar to Monday's Wootton game. Shio wanted to test our communication and in-game adjustments, so he controlled lineup changes and rotations while giving us various offensive attacks or looks on the opposing side of the court. There were setter dumps and tips but mostly outside hits.

Having Noah back was a godsend. All volleyball players know that feeling of having a reliable middle. It takes away the middle attack and slows down outside and right-side hits, making it easier for the defense to pass and transition if necessary.

Our next game was scheduled for Wednesday, April 25, 2018, against Bethesda Chevy Chase High School (B-CC for short). It was a home game, which was nice to have as we neared the end of the year.

Olivia going for an outside hit against B-CC.

On the day of the game, Shio decided to change the lineup to test our communication in game. At first I was hesitant because I didn't want us risking a set that would affect our ranking, but I trusted him and, initially, we went without Noah. The first set was much like that against Wootton. We struggled but not as badly as before. Some front-row attacks caught us off guard; however, we managed to pull away to win the first set.

In the second set, B-CC started to adjust to our plays more often. Noah missing a game was starting to show, as it took some time for him to get his body back in playing form. B-CC pulled away with a win to tie the set, 1-1. I went to Shio and urged him to stay with the original lineup to not risk any more sets and he agreed.

With our original starting lineup, we eased our way to win the next two sets and the game 3-1, bringing our overall record to 9-1. On one particular play B-CC had served a fast ball over the net. Tiffany, who was playing middle back, received it but it shanked off her hands and went flying to the main gym entrance just behind me. Not wanting to give up a free point, I sprinted as fast as I could toward the ball and did a bicycle kick in the air to send it back toward the net. Luckily, Noah was at the net to hit it over and earn us the point. As I stood up, I vividly remembered seeing everyone with their jaws to the floor. I couldn't believe what had happened either!

Our final game of the 2017-2018 year would be the following Monday, giving us a sizable portion of time to rest. We packed our things and headed home.

Chapter 24

Times of Joy and Happiness

Every season in sports is special in some way. It's not just about the wins or losses. Don't get me wrong, winning is really fun, but it's the memories you have along the way that truly make a season spectacular. I often looked back during my senior year to many moments throughout high school that at the time had felt commonplace. As I walked around Blair that final year, it triggered flashbacks to my earlier days as an underclassman. I would exit the gym hallway to the back of Blair and see my younger self walking home after volleyball practice every day along the sidewalk of Colesville Road. I would then turn and see the main back entrance to the school and see myself walking into high school for the first time. Each area of our campus felt like it had a story to tell me.

Our 2017-2018 season in particular was littered with moments throughout from the first time meeting each other to our last time as a team, which were some of the rarest and most spectacular experiences anyone could ever know.

One of the things about high school sports that was really fun was the bus rides to away games. Our bus rides on coed were unique adventures on their own. We held our own little live concerts of our favorite songs, at times even getting so loud that we could see passengers in cars turning their heads as we passed them on the road. We had conversations about the weirdest things and could make any minor instance into an unforgettable memory. We all had this chemistry that I couldn't make sense of. Somehow, our personalities and styles just blended really well together and, coupled with Shiotani's personality and coaching, created a recipe for happiness and fun.

Practices were another thing I always looked forward to. At times they could get really slow and repetitive, but we always found ways to make each other laugh and reenergize our spirits. Olivia would do her dance routine before serving, trying to make everyone laugh so they would mess up on serve receive. My cousin would talk trash and poke fun at people to try to get into their heads. Once, during a serving drill, Shio had me only serve my cousin just to irritate him. At one point I laughed so hard that he knew something was up and turned, only to see Shio instructing me to keep serving his way. Sometimes, we even held dodgeball games with Shio and Armstead. (Sorry about hitting you, Shio.) River started a game where you take your thumb and index finger a create a sort of circle. You had your hand below your waist and if someone looked at it you got them (or as it was said, "I got your neck.") Tyler would always end up hurting himself by attempting crazy dives or strange volleyball moves. (Some of which even found their way into games!)

Prior to practices, we would all line up against the gym hallway side of the main gym, prepping for practice. Every day as the team trickled into the gym, it was like adding ingredients to a pot, each increasing the flavor and richness of the recipe for coed. Everything was special about that year. I didn't want it to end, but as we neared the conclusion of the season, I slowly began to feel time ticking away.

I remember once I wanted to bring pizza for my cousin and some friends while we waited in Shio's room before practice. Of course at the time I didn't realize how big a mistake it was to bring pizza into a high school full of hungry students. As I stepped out of my car and walked toward Blair, I heard someone call me from a car. It was

Jaya. She called me over and asked for a slice. Having known Jaya for a long time, and given her position as a senior captain, I couldn't say no. I had to hide the pizza under my sweater the rest of the way to Shio's room.

I tried to open the door but it was locked. I glanced at my phone and realized that practice was minutes away from starting, so I sprinted as fast as I could toward the gym. Upon my arrival, Shio just gave me a confused look. As soon as I turned to sit down, the whole team was around me, asking for a slice. It's amazing how much power one has over others when they have food to give. I felt like a supervillain. I distributed whatever I could and got a lot of disappointed looks during the rest of practice.

It's crazy how everything that happened during our time together, and every story, no matter how little or big, ended up being an amazing tale to tell.

Our daily adventures to Four Corners were always fun and spontaneous. We talked about everything happening in our lives, be it work, school, relationships, or how much we hated running laps around the gym. On one occasion, coed was asked to work at the school concession stands one Friday night. Usually, each sport volunteered to handle the concessions during another sport's home game. It so happened that our day was a multi-header with girls softball, boys/girls lacrosse, and boys baseball all playing home games.

We manned the concession stand just at the entrance of the football stadium. My cousin Muhammad, Fiona, Avery, Olivia, Brenna, Tiffany, Tyler, Shio, and I were all there. It was a long day, but what made it such a cool experience and unforgettable memory in our lives was all of us being there together. We all cracked jokes about the season, and everyone asked about each other's future plans and childhood stories. Shio even let us eat snacks from the concession! It was such a fun day. At that moment I could feel the richness of life around me. I don't know what it was; maybe it was the realization that our journeys in high school were coming to an end. Maybe it was just one of those times in your life when things seem perfect and easy. Our conversations and debates about various topics were fun to be a part of. Debates about what was the greatest show on television split our team in half, but ultimately, it was all about celebrating the uniqueness of everyone on the team.

We seemed to have control over our own systems of functioning. When it was game time, we could get in the zone, and when it was time for fun, we went full-on goofball mode. I tried my best to somehow make sense of that little group of ours. I went back to that moment and how the whole season came about, starting with walking into Shio's room before the start of the season and talking about our upcoming plans. Outside of volleyball, I had no relationship with Elliott Shiotani nor did I have any connection whatsoever to anyone on the team except for my cousin, yet when I was with any of them, it was almost like I had spent my entire life with those people.

The month of April was nearing its end, which meant that our last day was fast approaching, but for the time being, I told myself I just needed to sit back and take in all the wondrous things that were happening around me; otherwise, I might miss them.

CHAPTER 25

The Beautiful Moments with Friends

Our last game of the 2017-2018 season was scheduled for Monday, April 30, 2018. It so happened that not only was it our last regular-season game but also our senior night. I found it very strange how that came about. The universe works in mysterious ways and sometimes all you can do is be grateful and marvel at all of it

Somehow, our schedule gave us the perfect conclusion to our long season. Normally, teams have their senior nights in the middle of the season. I remember one team even had theirs at an away game. Luckily, ours was a perfect conclusion to an epic season.

Practice leading up to our final game was more easy than usual. Shio wanted us to have a good time, given it was the last time seniors would play a regular season game. Although playoffs were right after, I'm glad he took the opportunity to give us our time to enjoy volleyball without having to worry about the upcoming game. We laughed throughout each practice. Every drill that began on a serious note ended with someone on the floor, dying with laughter. Everyone was making jokes and messing around with each other. At times we completely let go of our focus and forgot about volleyball-related things. Armstead was getting a little worried, given how serious she was about our team and the sport, but Shio calmed her down. Shio knew how special we were to each other, and he couldn't help but smile as he watched us goof around.

The Thursday before our last game, the long-awaited Marvel film, *Avengers: Infinity War*, was officially released in theatres. It had been 10 years in the making since the release of the first Iron Man movie. I was eight when the first Iron Man movie came out, and now I was almost 18 at the time of *Infinity War*. Time had flown by, just like that!

My friends and I scheduled to see it Friday after school. Friday was perfect, given it was the end of the week, and it being opening day meant a packed crowd with die-hard comic book fans. Noah had seen it the day before us and had a whole day of fun throwing out fake spoilers to everyone on our group chat.

"@Aziz Baig Thanos survives the movie 👀," Noah texted to the group chat.

Fiona, Jaya responded quickly with: "**Heyyyyyy spoilers**" and "**NO SPOILERS A**HOLES.**"

I myself pleaded: "**Noah don't do this.**"

Funny enough, much like how *Avengers: Infinity War* was a conclusion and celebration of 10 years of Marvel, our upcoming game was also a conclusion and celebration of sorts.

Each year, coed teams held an annual lunch visit to Four Corners for a sort of celebration of the season. In my final year we decided to head to Sweet Frog, which was a first. We almost forgot about it until Olivia reminded us. We planned to do it Friday, the 27th of April, but some people couldn't make it. I wanted it to be a special occasion and everyone had to be there, so we rescheduled for Monday before the game.

To fill the void of not having anything to do until then, River chimed in with a group poll, asking whether or not pineapple belonged on pizza, following with "Is water wet" and "Is fire burning?" polls. It got so real that different people were throwing in scientific evidence, logical reasoning, and clever ways of disproving each other. Those were the types of conversations that kept us up at night. Sure, they may have been conversations that ordinarily one might not seem to enjoy, but with us, anything we did together became something of a marvelous experience.

Friday's practice was a normal one. Since Monday was senior night, it was customary for all sports that, regardless of the original season-long lineup, coaches had seniors populate the starting positions as a nice way of sending them off before they graduated. The starting six for us, including the rotation players who subbed in, were mostly seniors, so we didn't have to change much. One thing Shio did was give us free rein to do whatever we wanted as long as it didn't cost us any sets or the game. "If we have a nice lead, go for it," said Shio when I asked him about jump serving.

Tyler also wanted to try jump serving. We practiced our jump serving with an excitement equivalent to a child being told they could finally drive their own car. At one point I mishit my jump serve and it curved to the left, almost hitting Shio. He just looked at me, and I knew he was asking himself whether or not he made a mistake giving us free rein for Monday's game.

We ended Friday's practice with a group huddle and mini speech. Shio thanked everyone for joining coed and for the amazing season thus far. He also gave seniors a round of applause for their hard work, and I must admit I got a little tear in my eye hearing him talk. Before it got too emotional, we broke the huddle and headed to get our gear and go home.

As we were packing our things, Fiona asked everyone except for seniors to stay back. The seniors gathered near our equipment and looked over. Fi was talking to the others about something. At the time we had no idea what it was, but we kept our eyes open for anything. At times we tried to decipher what they were saying by lip-reading, but they did a good job of keeping their conversation hidden from us. My cousin, who was in the huddle, walked back with a smile on his face. I tried my best to get the information out of him, but he wouldn't budge. Jaya and Brenna tried their best to bribe Fiona into telling them what their little meeting was about, but no one was talking.

Saturday morning I asked the group chat what the meeting without the seniors was about. Fiona simply responded with: **Uhhhh hangin out without you.**

They were doing a really good job of keeping their plans a secret. I was getting a little suspicious. My cousin asked if I could drop him off at Fiona's house that very weekend. My suspicions were immediately heightened because no one had told me about a gathering at Fiona's. He told me it was not for seniors, so I tried to hit him back with a trade-off. "I'll take you if you tell me what's going on." I got very close to breaking him, but at the last minute he assured me it was better if none of the seniors knew what was going on.

Sunday morning Fiona texted everyone: **"Hey seniors! As you probably know tomorrow is senior night. I'll have your spirit stuff in the morning, so please make sure to stop by outside the gym to pick it up before going to class."**

"Of course," I screamed. They were planning our senior night. *How could I not have figured this out?* To confirm, I asked for everyone's availability for our Monday Sweet Frog trip. Tyler wanted to do it Tuesday because of a test he had to study for. I poked fun at him, saying that the real reason he wanted to do Tuesday was so he had time to nap before the game. We all teased him and had a huge laugh about it. Tyler was known for being injury prone. His senior request was to play all rotations. We went over some last-minute things for senior night and called it a day.

Monday morning, the day of our final game of the regular season, was also the day after my 18th birthday. I felt really happy going to school that morning because of the game and the fact that I was no longer a kid. (Who am I kidding, I'm still a little kid.) But at the same time, I was sad because I knew my time at Blair was coming to an end. I dropped my backpack off in class and walked with Avery to find Fiona. They were standing just in front of the trophy case near the back entrance of the school, holding a large bag in their hand. Fiona handed us black T-shirts decorated with a galaxy theme. Each shirt had the words "CO-ED VOLLEYBALL SENIOR NIGHT 2018" on it with some decorations of spaceships, and behind them were our last names, jersey number, and the name of a planet. I loved them. In previous years we usually bought custom-made shirts online that were a little more official and professionally done, but they were very expensive, and it often caused much trouble to get them with individual customizations and then get the payments for all of them. What made the 2018 senior night shirts more special was the fact that they were simple and crafted by hand. The younger players had spent time and used their own talents to create works of art. Their handmade designs and creative artistic expressions were far more valuable than any professional custom-made shirt to us seniors.

Avery and I walked back to our class that morning and put them on, only to receive curious glances from everyone we passed in the hallways. The most awkward moment was walking into class that morning and hearing our teacher say, "I'm not even going to ask."

The final bell rang and off we went to set up for our game. As I got close to the gym entrance, I was stopped by some of the underclassmen. They were there to make sure the seniors did not enter until others had finished decorating. From what I could see, there were balloons in a multitude of colors, and the entrance to the gym was decorated with colorful strips of long paper.

We waited for them to allow us in, each second of waiting only increasing our anticipation. Because of how special that day was, and how much time we needed for speeches and player introductions, we decided to hold off on the Sweet Frog plan until Tuesday. When the underclassmen were ready, the seniors were given permission to enter the gym all together. We received cheers and screams from the team, coaches, and everyone sitting on the bleachers.

Before the match, Shio introduced us all individually. One by one we walked out with either friends or family to receive a rose and gift from Coach Armstead. My parents weren't at the game, so I had one of my best friends walk out with me. Shio stood with a microphone, reading off letters of appreciation the seniors had written.

A week earlier, Coach Armstead had made official senior night booklets that contained our season summary and player bios. On the front she had our school name, match details for senior night, and our group senior photo. The first page was dedicated to boys' volleyball with their roster and team picture. The next two pages had senior bios, our jersey numbers, position, plans after high school, athletic careers at Blair, and acknowledgments. That was followed by our roster and team picture. Armstead had even added a bonus section that included our team record, individual stats from our division championship game, and our division championship team photo.

Out in the hallway, the seniors had some time to talk to each other. Normally, we never discussed graduation or our last days of high school, but given the circumstances, we couldn't resist. I remember standing with everyone and we began to get a little emotional, realizing our moments together were fleeting. Shio's voice came over the speaker system. He started with a brief introduction of himself and Ms. Armstead and then the program. The spectators in the bleachers cheered and he continued with player introductions, each unique in its own way.

Shio spoke with eloquence, and his humor and smile brought radiance to the gym. Whenever he finished saying something, we all smiled as we watched. When it came to my turn, he paused. There come times in your life when you meet people who are special, and I don't just mean perfect. There is something about them that you often ask yourself how it was that you met them in the first place. Elliott Shiotani was one of those people for me. A man I never knew prior to coed volleyball would become someone I would forever cherish as of the most amazing human beings I have met in my life. I knew our bond was a special one, especially with coed.

Shio took a long pause and snuck in a little joke, as he always did to keep the mood light. Then he read the letter of appreciation I had emailed him as a way of thanking everyone. Next he did something I will never forget. Shio gave me a heartfelt congratulations and thanks for everything I had done for coed. "He promised me he'd bring coed a division title before he was done with it, and he did," Shio ended.

As I walked out I had to hold back my tears. I went up to him and hugged him as hard as I could and whispered in his ear, "Thanks, Shio."

We grabbed our roses and gift bags and took pictures individually, then as a team. As Shio named us off one by one, emotions slowly began creeping in. Reminders of the journey we had been on and our time together under this ceiling were flashing before us. It was such an awesome experience that I nearly forgot we had a game that day. And if I'm being honest, I didn't want any of it to end. Not just that day but the season. I didn't want to know a life without these people and volleyball in it.

We wrapped up senior night celebrations and quickly transitioned to game-time preparations.

Coed volleyball seniors on senior night.

Coed volleyball seniors on senior night with Mrs. Johnson.

Coed on senior night.

Seniors with their families

Our opponent that night was Watkins Mill High School. In that game we didn't worry about records or playoffs, we just wanted to have a good time together on the court. Shio submitted his lineup and the match was set to start. I called everyone over for a huddle and gave what would be my last speech for a regular-season game at Blair. "Alright, guys, this is it, our last regular-season game and senior night. Remember your fundamentals and communication but don't forget to enjoy tonight. Let's go out there and have some fun. Smile! Be loud! Cheer each other on! Let's give everyone a night to remember!" I said, and we broke the huddle.

As always we won the coin toss and elected to serve first. Shio gave us the thumbs up and we were off. Our energy that night was through the roof. By that point in the season, we had played long enough with each other that we blended together perfectly. Our chemistry was at an all-time high. We had a rich understanding of each other's playing styles and communicated clearly. We stuck to our base positions and executed plays with perfection. Watkins Mill was no match for us that night. Tyler and I even got to jump serve. Before I did it, Shio looked over at me and said, "Make sure it goes in at least," with a smile on his face.

Everyone was enjoying themselves. Our volleyball play was filled with excitement and ease. The home crowd was getting louder by the play. It was a quick game, one of our smoother ones. We cruised to a 3-0 victory against Watkins Mill.

Watching from the sidelines during our senior night game against Watkins Mill.

Brenna going for a hit against Watkins Mill.

Getting ready on defense during our senior night game against Watkins Mill.

Coed getting ready for the next point against Watkins Mill on senior night

As the final whistle blew, we jumped and cheered louder than ever. There were laughs and a lot of crying. Parents and friends came down to greet us. It was truly something amazing to witness. Mrs. Johnson, our school principal, was also in attendance. She came over and congratulated us and even took a team picture with us. It was an amazing night and one that I will never forget.

We left Blair that day with smiles as wide as the distance between the East and West coasts. We walked back to our cars, comforted by the fact that we had just had the most successful season in coed volleyball history at Blair but also hopeful for what was to come. Our overall record stood at 10-1, locking up the third spot in the Montgomery County rankings. We got home and continued to celebrate through texts. I thanked the underclassmen for an absolutely wonderful and well-planned senior night. It was certainly the best one I could recall in my memory at Blair.

For the first time in a long time, we had a night to ourselves to enjoy and fully soak in the successful season we'd had. I must admit it was difficult to sleep. I couldn't stop thinking about how lucky we were to have the season go the way it did, but I knew it didn't end there. The next day would bring the start of a new chapter in our lives. One that would put all the cards on the line and one that could cement our legacy among the all-time greats at Blair. Playoffs had arrived.

Chapter 26

Isn't It So Sweet?

Tuesday after the game we were anticipating a return to our regularly scheduled practice to start getting ready for the playoffs. Everyone waited after school for an email or some hint about our schedule. Then Shiotani texted me about canceling practice. We all felt a bit down about that, but our frozen yogurt trip would come to save the day. Everyone met in the gym hallway. Some people had a ninth period, so we had to wait a while in Shio's room. Jaya and Brenna were already waiting for us. Some players couldn't come, which immediately prompted those who were coming to brand them "fake."

There was an awards ceremony scheduled for Wednesday, which I assumed was the annual sports awards ceremony Blair had started doing two years prior, but it turned out to be some other awards ceremony. Shio informed us we were also scheduled to work the concessions stand that same night, so everyone went into panic mode thinking we had a back-to-back packed schedule.

We departed from the gym hallway and walked to Four Corners together. The weather was beautiful that day, with nothing but golden sunshine and a light breeze. Frozen Yogurt—or Froyo as it was known in the area—was this little ice cream shop just in front of Blair. It was a popular spot for students to head to after school. Inside, you could grab any size cup you wanted and had total freedom to pick any flavor along with whatever topping you liked. The only thing, though, was you had to watch how heavy the cup was because it directly affected how much it was going to cost.

Half the team had paid for their frozen yogurt, and just as I finished paying for mine, Shio walked in and informed everyone he was going to pay for all the frozen yogurts. We all got so angry, especially considering he told my cousin to let the entire team know about it ahead of time but my cousin had somehow forgotten to let us know. Only half the team got frozen yogurt for free, any size cup with however much in it they wanted.

We sat outside together, occupying all the round tables in groups and talked about the season. That was, of course, after we finished lashing out at my cousin for not remembering to tell us about Shio offering to pay for everyone. We went over what we had done right and what we could've worked on better.

Seniors told everyone where they were going and what they were going to study after graduation. Seniors were firmly split down the middle between Maryland and California. Tyler and I would be attending college in Maryland while the rest—Avery, Tiffany, Jaya, Noah, and Brenna—were all headed to California. Hours must have passed, but it felt like minutes. It was nice to sit down and chat about life for a change. That was one of the most amazing things about high school. It was that time in your life when things weren't certain but you were figuring it out along the way and discovering your place in the world. It was one of the more peaceful days at Blair during that season.

It was getting late so we called it day and walked back together to Blair. We said our goodbyes and went home.

Chapter 27

The Next One After

Montgomery County announced that the first round of play-offs for coed volleyball would begin on Thursday, May 3, 2018, which gave us only one day of practice before the game. It also happened to be the same day we had to run the concessions for lacrosse, softball, and baseball after our practice.

Based on the rankings, our first opponent would be Wootton High School, which we had played against in week nine, winning 3-1. Although we had beaten them on their court, anything was possible in the playoffs, especially now that they had a full game of experience against us. We also had stats on their games as well, so we knew exactly what to work on. Coach Armstead kept every stat sheet for all of our games.

Wednesday's practice would be heavily influenced by the previous Wootton game, the only difference being that now we had Noah the second time around. He was the ace up our sleeve they didn't know about. We ran our normal offense and defense during practice, this time much more smoothly now that middle was dealt with by Noah. Jaya and Fiona ran their setter rotations with hitters running all three spots in the front row. The defense was working on those outside attacks that had got us last time we played Wootton. Tyler, Avery, and Tiffany were controlling their parts of the court. Because the boy's season was over, we had the luxury of having the whole gym to ourselves, giving us two nets to work with and two carts of balls. There was one catch, however. Having the whole gym meant that shagging volleyballs was much more difficult.

Volleyball players are all too familiar with shagging balls after a drill. Shagging balls refers to the act of collecting all the balls after a drill and placing them in the ball carts. Shio would initiate shagging by counting down from ten, at times even intentionally throwing the balls back out that we had already put in the cart. If every ball was not in the carts by the time he finished counting, we had to do conditioning.

Shio and Armstead worked us until we could barely move. Playoff atmospheres were much more intense than regular games, so we had to be sure to cover any possible situations that might occur.

To mimic those playoff scenarios which can induce anxiety and panic in an athlete, Armstead and Shio would call out a game situation. For example, they would say, "Okay, you and Wootton are tied two to two. This is the fifth set, both teams tied at ten, last five points to win the game." They also came up with this unique system where different colored balls meant different things. White was a normal ball that we could choose to play however we wanted. Blue was a shanked pass, giving us only two plays on the ball, and red was a situation in which a girl had to be the last one to send the ball over the net to simulate coed rules. As they threw the ball at us, they would cover its color, and we had to watch for it in the air and call what play it was. It was an excellent way to not only work on communication but also work on transitions and quick thinking in game-time situations. It's easy in practice to make a mistake and run it over again, but when it comes to real games, once a point is over there's no getting it back, so it was vital to give each ball our full effort.

We ended practice on a six on six scrimmage and called it a day. Because it was the first playoff game of the season, and a home game at that, Shio wanted to make sure we were doing the right kinds of preparations before Thursday. "Drink lots of water, keep your body relaxed and ready. Please don't eat any junk food or do anything that could get you hurt." He looked directly at Tyler as he said that. "Tomorrow's a big day, so everyone needs to be on time. And let's get this win. Let's get a Blair on three and head over to concessions."

Some players left for home because of how far away they lived, but those of us who were in close proximity to Blair and didn't have to worry about our homework for the night stayed back to run concessions. My cousin, Avery, Tiffany, Tyler, Olivia, Fiona, Brenna, and Shio were all there. Ms. Boule set up two tables just inside the entrance to the football stadium. There were snacks and drinks (which we ate with Shio's permission of course). Lacrosse was having their senior night, so boys and girls varsity were on the football field. Boys baseball was having a game, as well as girls softball. The crowd that night was massive. Normally at Blair, only football games drew that large of a crowd.

For the most part, we talked to each other about what was going on in our lives. I happened to be watching the girls softball game because I knew they were having a great season. At the time they were down 9-0, heading toward the end of the game. We all watched as they slowly came from behind to win 12-11. High school has something to it that is very rare, a sense of togetherness. Everyone is part of one community under a single roof, and that night was one of those moments we all came together and supported each other as a community and school. There were cheers throughout the night coming from all directions. We met and talked with friends as they dropped by the concession stands.

It got very late and most of the team had gone home. Shio, my cousin, and I were among the last ones to leave. He asked us how we felt going into the playoff game. I told him how excited I was about it. It was exciting to be playing past the regular season and knowing we had a team that could actually make a run. Our season had been good and all, but if we didn't do anything in the playoffs, then it would all have gone to waste. I must admit there was a part of me that was nervous about the game. I wasn't as worried about losing as I was about how I was going to play.

On Thursday, May 3, 2018, I awoke with extreme excitement for our playoff game against Wootton High School. We had some time to ourselves before the game because coed softball was hosting its final game of the season in the main gym. Avery, Tiffany, my cousin, and I swung by Four Corners to pick up some Slurpees before the game. Coming back, we met Coach Armstead outside the main gym entrance and talked about lineups and our plans for the game. Shio was inside with the rest of the team, so we joined them and watched coed softball for a while. My friends also joined us to help work.

For playoffs, students who worked volleyball games got paid by the school, so that was an offer they couldn't resist. In the final minutes of the coed softball game, Shio signaled everyone to run warmups in the small gym. We changed and did a light warm-up then proceeded with individual drills. I worked on passing and hitting with my cousin. Tyler, Avery, and Tiffany ran their three-person passing drill. Jaya and Fiona were setting back and forth between each other. Noah was working on his hitting against the wall, along with Brenna. Everyone else was scattered about, running various drills. All you could hear was the sound of shoes hitting the floor as the players ran and dozens of volleyballs bouncing up and down.

While warming up, I was reminded of a story that Coach Chris and the boy's team had told me. During a home playoff for boys' varsity, my cousin had been one of the line judges for Blair. It was customary for coed and boys to occupy working positions for each other during home games. On one particular play, Blair hit a ball near the outer boundary of the court; however, it was difficult to see whether or not it had landed in or out. The entire gym, including the referee, was looking at my cousin to make the call, given he was closest to it. In a state of utter confusion, he impulsively called that the ball was out, which led to an outcry on the boy's side for Blair. My cousin would later admit that he had been daydreaming during the play so he decided to make a random call—which ended up being wrong. Chris and the boys all jumped in frustration because they knew they had lost a point. After the game they had a big laugh about it, and I always remembered that funny moment from time to time when I needed something to ease my worries.

—⚡—

Softball finished their game so we headed back inside the main gym and began setting up. The music was on high volume and playoffs were underway. The referees walked in along with Wootton. They wore all black that day. Their demeanor reflected extreme focus and determination. They were out to avenge their regular season loss. We, on the other hand, were jamming to songs playing through the speakers and having the time of our lives. Everyone was relaxed and ready to go.

The refs called captains over. This time there were two refs, one who stood at the top of the net in the normal referee spot and another who was at the opposite end of the net to help out with close calls. Usually, in regular-season games for coed, there was only one ref, which could be both a good and a bad thing, depending on how you looked at it. It could be a benefit for your team because having two sets of eyes could mean more calls would be made correctly now that a second referee had a better vantage point to see plays that were difficult for the main referee to call. It also meant that fouls—like net violations and such—that sometimes didn't get whistled for during games could now be called more often. That can hurt a team, because it means both teams have to be careful not to commit unnecessary fouls that give away free points.

We won the coin toss and elected to serve.

I called everyone over during warmups and warned them to be more vigilant about the referees. There are times during games when teams may have players cross the middle line but the referee was occupied elsewhere on the court. With two refs, we had to be careful to not make those same mistakes and risk crucial points. Another thing was to follow the ball all the way through, no matter how close it seemed to be going in or out.

Wootton warmed up first. As I watched them execute plays, it was clear they had improved greatly since we last saw them. As we warmed up after Wootton, I occasionally looked over at their side to see their reactions to how we were playing. I could tell they were perplexed by Noah, not having seen him before. Whenever he swung hard and got a middle kill, their eyes would light up. We ended with serves and went back to our side of the court.

Armstead and Shio pulled us aside out in the hallway to give us some motivation before the game. They instructed us to forget about both teams' records and the fact that we beat them before. We were two different teams since we last met. "Focus on what you can control. Stay calm, it's just another volleyball game. Communicate with each other and remember your fundamentals," said Shio. It wasn't anything we hadn't heard before, but this time we seemed to hear his words more clearly. The playoffs were very nerve wracking, but somehow Shio found a way to bring us all back down to earth and instill confidence in us.

He submitted the lineup and we were off. I held a mini huddle like always, and Jaya and I went over our points of emphasis for the game. We needed to start strong and keep the lead. We needed to make Wootton earn their points, and we had to stop their offensive attacks while giving our setters a good pass. And we needed to finish plays strong.

We started the match as planned. Earning some early points, we slowly built a lead, forcing Wootton to call a timeout. They were struggling with Jaya's serving until, finally, they made a rotation play where they hid their weak passer.

Having Noah really changed the game for us. Now that middle was taken care of, we could reorient our focus to their outside hitters. Front-row players like Avery and me took care of their outside hits while Brenna stuffed their middle attacks. Jaya and Fiona were setting the ball with ease. Our team was unstoppable. Wootton tried their best to break our momentum, but with every play they took from us, we responded with greater intensity. They had no answer for us, and we cruised to a 3-0 victory. . On the last play Tyler even snuck in a perfect ace from a jump serve! We shook hands with Wootton. They showed the utmost level of class and sportsmanship, and that was truly something special. Their coaches congratulated us and we went our separate ways.

We gathered on our side of the court in a big circle. No one could control their excitement. Shio congratulated Noah for his outstanding game, and we all cheered for him. Shio and Armstead quickly went over the stats for the game and told us what to think about at practice the next day.

Ms. Boule was in attendance and also came down to congratulate us. It had been a long time since a coed volleyball team at Blair had not only made the playoffs but survived the first round. She gave us some words of encouragement and went her way. We packed and took down the nets. As I walked back and forth between the gym and equipment room to unpack things, I could hear teammates talking about various plays made during the game. There were mentions of kills from Olivia, Brenna, Avery, Noah, and me. People were amazed by the defense from Tyler, Tiffany, and Avery, and the immaculate sets from Jaya and Fiona. I knew it was short-lived, but we had a night to enjoy our win because next it was back to practice and on to the next game.

I drove home with my cousin to the sound of music pouring from our windows. We pulled into the driveway of our house, attracting the attention of many heads as we passed by. Our parents could tell by the way we walked in that we had won. I went to my room and dropped dead on my bed. I laid there, staring at the ceiling, still not able to accept that we had won a playoff game. At this point during the previous two years, we had been celebrating the conclusion of our season, so it felt weird yet exciting to still be playing volleyball past the regular season's conclusion.

I had flashbacks of the game all night. Every corner I turned and every movement I made in the house reminded me of something that had transpired in the game. I would smile at times as I mimicked spiking the ball in the air as I walked around the house, drawing confused looks from family members.

Our group chat was ecstatic. Everyone was in shock because of our win. I got notifications from Twitter about Mr. Fong, Blair athletics, and Mrs. Johnson tweeting the playoff win. They even had a video of Tyler's game-winning serve to go along with the catchy phrases and heartfelt congratulations. I called it day and went to bed.

Chapter 28

I Can't Believe We're Here

Friday morning after the game, River decided to begin our day with another philosophical question. "What goes in the bowl first, milk or cereal?" she asked.

To screw around with everyone, I argued for milk going in first, which led to a great deal of shock and memorable reactions.

"Aziz, I respect you so much and then you come out with this sh*t wrote Noah.

"I say the bowl comes first," wrote Olivia.

The thought of having another repetitive practice could be tiresome at times, but those kinds of conversations always kept the mood fun and joyful. No matter the circumstance, we always found a way to keep each other smiling so that when the time came to play volleyball, the environment would be one where everyone could thrive and feel energized.

Friday's practice started with Coach Armstead going over the stats for the game. She had three sheets of white paper, one for each set. There were circles drawn, underlines made, different uses of color, and writing all over. She broke down each set in detail, making sure to celebrate each successful play and calling out our mistakes. For the most part we had dominated all aspects of the game; however, there were minor errors we had made that could come back to haunt us later in the playoffs against better teams.

MCPS Athletics announced Friday that the next round of playoffs would take place on Tuesday, May 8, 2018. Based on the current playoff standings, our next opponent was Walter Johnson, who we had played to open the season. Like Wootton, they were now a much different team than when we first met them, and the fact that they were in the second round of the playoffs meant they were a strong team that had a successful season of their own. Their home opening loss to Blair also added fuel to their thirst for revenge.

We had three days of practice, giving us adequate time to rest up. For three days we ran drills over and over again, even though we ran them well. Shio and Armstead wanted to keep our focus on fundamentals in the hopes that it was something we could refer to in case things went sideways during a game. As an athlete, physical skills can only take you so far, and like anything in life, there's a limit to what those skills can do for you. It was important that we also prioritized keeping up with the mental aspects of our preparation.

During one of our usual drills, we let a ball drop untouched on the court two plays in a row. "Why is everyone standing? If this next ball hits the court untouched, we're running ladders," said Shio with a serious look on his face.

The same went for serving. To add pressure and recreate the atmosphere of an actual game, Shio and Armstead had us line up and serve at designated spots on the court. If the drill proved too difficult, they altered it a little and, instead, asked for any kind of serve, so long as it went over the net. If a serve went out on the opposite side of the court, everyone had to do pushups, but if the ball didn't even make it to the other side of the net, we would run ladders and do conditioning.

Practices normally lasted two hours, but they started to feel like four with the intensity of our workouts. I can still recall the looks of tired and sweaty faces gasping for air as each drill came to a close. Earlier in the year, we may not have been able to deal with the added workload, but our desire to win counties gave us an extra bit of energy to push through. We'd often stare at the coed volleyball banner, which was situated just above our heads, and focus on its emptiness to remind ourselves what was at stake in the upcoming days and weeks.

On Tuesday I arrived early at school, wearing my jersey. Gamedays were particularly difficult as a student because all I could think about during class was volleyball-related things. During lunch, I went over to Shio's room to talk about the game as a way to ease my nerves and get out whatever thoughts or feelings I had so that I could be more focused during class. I always found it comforting to speak with him about anything. Somehow, he always kept his cool and never showed any nerves.

I asked him about lineups and such. He told me what he heard about how other schools did in the playoffs in case we met them in the future, but more importantly, he stressed keeping my priorities with school and my personal life in check. During the season, an athlete can become so focused on just sports-related things that they may not give enough of their time to other endeavors, but part of being a student athlete, or a human, is learning to live a balanced life and understanding the responsibility of keeping up with the many roles one carries.

At the sound of the final bell, some of us waited in Shio's room before the game. We had a couple of hours to ourselves to do whatever we wanted, but given our impatience, we wanted to start warming up as quickly as possible. We set up the net and began working on some hitting lines and base defense.

Some time went by and more people began trickling into the main gym. Walter Johnson arrived in their white uniforms adorned with green numbers. Although we had been told not to on countless occasions, we had this habit of carefully observing every player on the opposing side to not only guess who would be on the starting rotation but to analyze which players were good at doing various things we needed to take note of. (Sorry, Coach Armstead!) We made sure to note any tall players or ones who could hit consistently so as to adjust our defense accordingly.

The buzzer rang and warmups started. I worked on my hitting against the wall and then did some peppering with my cousin along the divider of the gym. I would look over between breaks at the Walter Johnson side and study their players individually on my own. I wanted to see how they played and did specific things like passing or setting.

During my first two years of coed, one thing I noticed was that I went into every game blind. I did not know who on the other side could hit, serve, or pass, and that lack of information was significant, as it could have helped greatly with our adjustments (which would come too late after the opening set). I made it another one of my little goals to be proactive when it came to preparing for another team. In any sport, if you watch a group of players long enough, you can form a case conceptualization of sorts. It can be helpful to learn about player habits or tendencies.

In volleyball some important things to look for were how comfortable the setter looked with setting the outside, middle, and right sides and how good or accurate the passers were. With hitters, it was important to look for things like consistency, accuracy, and power. I would watch to see which players on opposing teams could not only hit consistently in one position but hit in different positions and whether or not their hits were powerful.

Captains were called. I whispered to Jaya that we were going to win the coin toss, and I was right again. That had to be some kind of record or something. We elected to serve.

We ran our team warm-up after Walter Johnson, being watched by their players who were preoccupied with one goal: beating us to avenge their home-opening loss.

Coed warming up before our second playoff game against Walter Johnson.

Coach Armstead and Shio tried each game to discourage us from watching other teams, but we insisted it was something we needed to do to get some idea of who we were facing. Although we had played them earlier in the year, Walter Johnson had changed since then and were a completely different team heading into that playoff game. It was clear they had improved every aspect of their team.

Tyler and Avery were standing next to me as we broke down everything we saw. Tyler said to take note of where their hitters were mostly hitting. They had multiple tall middle players, so Noah and Brenna had to be on the lookout for a lot of middle sets. Their defense was also very strong in receiving serves and hits, but here and there we noticed players who seemed nervous.

We lined up on our end line to get ready to shake hands. As we exchanged our expressions of sportsmanship while clapping the Walter Johnson players, I remember seeing the look in each of the Walter Johnson player's eyes. They weren't very warm and friendly like at the home opener. They had eyes of determination and unhindered confidence.

Before the match started I called everyone over. That year I had found myself more of a captain than in previous years. I usually liked to take a back seat and let Jaya or Shio do the pep talks, but that year I wanted to take on the leadership position Shio had entrusted me with. "Okay, guys, here we are again. We've already played them once, but forget about that game. That was a long time ago. Let's just worry about each other. Always communicate. I want to hear everyone yell as loud as they can on the floor today. If you make a mistake, shake it off and support each other. The score is always zero to zero. Let's get a Blair on three and show them what Blair is made of."

The game started with a back-and-forth exchange of points. No team had a clear advantage. We would serve over, they'd receive and get a kill, and vice versa. Middles were going at each other. Noah and Brenna exchanged some blocks with Walter Johnson players. I was getting kills along with Avery and Olivia, but Walter Johnson responded right back with their own. The score was close until we pulled away in the end, thanks to our serving aces.

The second set was no different than the first. It was a constant battle and trading of points. Both teams looked determined to outwit the other. At times things got pretty heated on the court. Jaya with her rock-solid composure brought us all together and recentered our focus. She mentioned that one of their passers seemed to have been masked during serves. In volleyball a team can shift or transition one of their front row players back as a passer, allowing a weak passer to "hide" behind three other players who are ideally stronger passers (although all four can interact with the serve). Jaya told us to aim our hits and serves at that one individual. For the next handful of points, we targeted their weak passer on defense. With some help from aces and direct outside kills, we pulled away to go up 2-0.

Although we were winning, the game felt completely the opposite way. We were winning sets just points away from Walter Johnson. It is common in volleyball for momentum to suddenly shift, giving a team the needed energy for a comeback, even down 2-0. Walter Johnson caught on to our offensive strategy. They subbed their weaker passer out for another player. The substitution would prove to be crucial, as it greatly bolstered their previously exposed defense. Having a strong defense, along with a strong serve receive, put pressure on our offense and servers.

The only way to counter a team with a strong defense and serve receive is to either get direct kills/aces or hope for a mistake on their part. Walter Johnson had the edge over us for the entire set. Our kills were being blocked or well received, and they quickly transitioned off defense into quick attacks. Slowly, our communication and base defense broke down. We were tired and made a lot of mental mistakes. They pulled away to win the set, making it 2-1.

The momentum was slowly starting to shift. Walter Johnson was getting louder by the second. Shio and Armstead pulled us aside and told everyone to relax and take a deep breath. We had to trust in our abilities and communicate more. Transitions needed to be made faster, and hitters—like me—needed to find weak spots on the court to aim at.

As I looked over at the bleachers, I saw many familiar faces. My best friends were in attendance, along with Ms. Boule, Mr. Fong, and other parents. They slowly started cheering and rocking the bleachers by kicking them. It sounded like an earthquake. Unbeknownst to our fans, they had given us the energy boost we needed.

Before the fourth set, I called everyone over and emphasized simplifying the game. "Let's not do anything fancy. We've been practicing this all year long. Let's stick to simple plays, keep the ball in, and don't give them free points. Noah, show their middles who's boss. Avery and Tyler, talk to Tiffany about your defensive positions. Jaya, let us know where you need us to be, and Liv, you and I need to start smarter." We broke the team huddle with renewed energy and passion.

Walter Johnson served over. Tyler passed a perfect ball to Jaya, who set me on the outside. Rather than hitting to the middle position, I redirected my arm swing and went down the line directly in front of me. It went in and everyone jumped and cheered. Slowly, we fought our way to a nice lead. Noah took care of their middle, leaving that part of the defense covered. Liv was hitting various spots, confusing their defense. Noah and Brenna were running middle sets with Jaya that were very effective. To stop the bleeding, Walter Johnson called timeout.

Their timeout would prove crucial, as it defused our energy and slowed the game down. We fought until the score was tied in the 20s. We went ahead a couple of points, but Walter Johnson was slowly closing in. With the score at 24-22, Walter Johnson had the ball and served. I could hear our bench quickly yell, "IN!" and then a second later yell, "OUT." I watched as the ball floated its way out, giving us the 3-1 win. We all jumped and cheered.

As I walked down the net to shake hands with the Walter Johnson players, their coach gave me personal congratulations and complimented my hitting. I thanked him, and we exchanged some post-game laughs and went our separate ways.

We huddled on our side of the court, beaming with excitement and sweat. Shio let Armstead talk and quickly go over stats. They were most proud of our resilience and team effort when things got really tough. Usually, a game like that would be a cause for celebration, but it was clear we had plenty of mistakes to fix. They congratulated us and we took down the nets and headed home.

I arrived home with my phone bursting with notifications from everyone. Twitter was screaming with tweets and retweets of our win, with videos of the final play as well as one of my hits from the second set. Blair sports wrote on their post, "Coed Volleyball with the win!! Game, set, match! On to the final four!" I became fixated on the last part of that tweet: "final four." Those words seemed to really give me perspective on how far we had made it into the playoffs. With just two more wins, we could be county champions.

As I changed and prepared for bed, Olivia texted everyone with updates from the rest of the county. "Churchill beat Rockville. Going onto Clarksburg Friday."

Avery chimed in, informing us that Sherwood had also won their game, meaning the top four remained unchanged. We ended the day reassuring each other of our potential and enjoyed the win for a short time.

The next game was on our doorstep. Sherwood was up next!

Chapter 29

At the End of a Chapter

Montgomery County scheduled the next round of the semi-final playoff games for Thursday, May 10, 2018, giving us only one day of rest and practice. We had hoped for some more time off to reset ourselves and work on our mistakes, but given the way the schedule had been set up, the last day for seniors was toward the end of May, which meant our game had to be played before then (also factoring in the county championship game as well). With how the seedings and playoffs turned out, our next opponent was Sherwood. Churchill was to play Clarksburg, with the winners of both games meeting for the county championship.

We met before practice in Shio's room. The usual smile on his face was absent. As we walked to the gym, Shio had his duffle over his shoulder and did not utter a single word, which was not his usual attitude. As I walked through the gym doors, I had never heard it so quiet before. Usually, there was music playing, the echoes of everyone talking, or the thumping of a dozen volleyballs striking the ground or gym walls, but today all that greeted us was silence.

Prior to the start of practice, Shio called everyone in for a huddle, which was not his usual habit. "Okay, guys, this next game is a big one. I want everyone to be at their best today. Give it your all and leave everything on the court. Remember our loss against Sherwood this year. We have a chance to not only beat them but secure a spot in counties. Let's get a Blair on three and make this our best practice yet!"

For the entire season, we'd had our laughs and good times, but our next game was no joke. It was personal. Sherwood had always beaten Blair going back years, and Shio had never beaten them in his tenure as the coach for coed volleyball. I had lost to Sherwood all three times I played them. The common thread between all the games was how easily Sherwood swept Blair. Those losses became forever imprinted in my memory.

Now we had a chance to not only get revenge for our loss to them in week two of the 2017-2018 season but a chance to take out one of the all-time great programs in the county and qualify for a spot in the county championship game, which would be a first in school history.

We set up the nets and were called over for another huddle before practice started. Shio and Armstead made it abundantly clear that this practice had to be our best one if we wanted to beat Sherwood. I had never seen both our coaches so serious before, but I understood where they were coming from. I personally was a part of those gruesome defeats to Sherwood the last two years and was in no mood to have it happen again, especially after all we had been through that season.

Practice started with a quick stretch and then peppering. Jaya and I extended the expectations from Shio and Armstead. We made sure to be loud and disciplined during drills. Of course we couldn't contain our joy and playfulness, which was a big part of our personality as a whole. As a captain, or even just an individual really, you have to find a way to always be in a state of balance. If you're too serious about something then you end up losing joy for it, but if you're too loose and playful then you can lose hard work and seriousness. Every play we made was met with commentary and advice from all around. Perfection was our aim, and we were not stopping until we got there or as close as we possibly could.

I remember that during my first year with coed, Shio and I weren't aware of who Sherwood High School was when it came to volleyball. Shio knew them from his field hockey coaching experience and that was the extent of it. Blair would come to know Sherwood as the immovable obstacle every year. It was our first go around with volleyball, and we were just entering our first ever game of the year, playing an away game at Sherwood. Our practices were very lax and in a trial phase. We didn't have a schedule or strict script to follow, and the entire year was a reflection of our inexperience. Over time we slowly developed a consistent schedule, and I could see the growth coed had made, but it all had to start from ground zero. We were beaten very badly at Sherwood, and that would forever change our perception of the sport. It really was a turning point for Blair because we had never competed on such a level, and if we as a program wanted to get to that level then everything about Blair had to change.

The culture of coed was always one of a fun and nonserious sport. It was never competitive and there weren't any expectations or goals set. When Shio stepped in, the first thing he did was change the culture around the sport. No longer was it just about having fun; it became about winning. Slowly, it garnered support from Blair, and more players joined over time, not just first-timers but experienced players who initially forwent the season because it was considered a joke sport. Shio then brought in some experience with Ms. Armstead, and they built a system around the sport, one that could develop young players and utilize experienced players to build a strong team. Their efforts showed as Blair went from a two-win season to a four-win season and then a ten-win season. In a weird way, we had Sherwood to thank for our turnaround.

Practice lasted over two hours on Wednesday. Each minute was used to its absolute max with minimal time for jokes. The entire school was mostly empty by that point. All you could hear were the sounds of shoes screeching on the floor and balls making contact with the floor. During hitting drills, it didn't matter how perfect our hits were, they were never good enough for us. Every approach had to be given its all, and each hit had to be harder than the last. On defense I could see the frustration on everyone's faces. One mistake deflated everyone.

Serving was where things got really detailed. Shio had us run serves, and every miss meant doing pushups. Serving is usually something we were solid at, but knowing we were playing away, and with Sherwood's low ceiling, we had to push ourselves more. By the end of it all, we were exhausted beyond anything. Sweat was dripping from everyone and all you could hear was heavy breathing.

We ended practice with some playoff game situations. Playing Sherwood meant the sets would either be close or we would be down, so Shio put us in situations we had been in during previous Sherwood games. "Alright, you guys are down zero to five. Get those five points back," he stated and ultimately worked his way through the whole set. "The set is now tied twenty a piece. Finish those last five, and don't give them anything!" he said loudly.

We finished with some more game scenario situations and called it a day. Now even more drenched in sweat, and barely standing on two feet, everyone gathered around their equipment to gulp down water as fast as they could. Shiotani and Armstead came over and gave everyone some instructions. Things like staying hydrated and not doing anything dangerous at home (at which point we all looked at Tyler, knowing his antics). Nets were taken down and we all left the gym with the possibility that it could be our last official practice and last time in the gym together.

When I arrived home I went straight to my phone and texted everyone, "Tomorrow is it, guys." I wanted to keep our mental side of the game strong, and issuing a reminder of what was on the line seemed fitting. We all went back and forth about what to wear for spirit. It needed to be something special, given the occasion, so we ultimately decided to wear our jerseys. It was simple but symbolic for us. Jaya didn't want to overcomplicate things and felt that the jerseys were a nice way to stay focused and represent Blair proudly.

Throughout the season I had kept the pregame coin toss ritual that I did with Jaya a secret. The Sherwood game was the first time I announced the ritual to the whole team. "I'm calling it. We're getting serve first set," I texted.

A little surprised, Jaya responded, "You've never done it that way before. What if you jinxed it?"

She was probably right, but the entire season had been magical, and I wanted to share our little pre-game magic with the rest of the team. Before our conversations bled into our precious nap time, everyone logged off their phones.

I must be honest in that it was very difficult to sleep that night. Nights before a game were a strange time for me, not because I was nervous about winning but because I always worried about how I was going to play. I was always worried that if I didn't play well, it could negatively impact the team. Athletes know this experience all too well. You can get locked in a whirlpool of thoughts about things in the future. You ask yourself hypothetical scenario-based questions and wonder how things will play out, but ultimately, your mind will never be satisfied until it's game time.

For much of my life, I grew up watching leaders take charge of their teams and lead them to victory, but when you step into their shoes, you get to experience a little more than what you see watching others. Captains and leaders carry a great burden on their shoulders. They have expectations from everyone, and if those aren't met, it can take a toll on them, not to mention the team as a whole. It was the first time all year that I was actually worried about losing. I knew how good Sherwood was and how easily they beat us the first time around. It was also an away game, which added another element to it. Just like my coed journey began at Sherwood, it could also end at Sherwood. What goes around comes around, right?

—w—

It was the morning of Thursday, May 10, 2018. My friends expressed interest in coming to the game, as well as my dad. I decided to drive them and not take the bus because none of them had any means of transportation. I now look back at that moment and ask myself if it was the right thing to do. Sure, it was nice that I got to drive my friends to the game, but I missed out on a bus ride that was the arguably the most important of my career. I was not there for my friends and coaches, and I couldn't imagine what was going through their heads.

The other members of the team met up in the gym hallway and they all took the bus. My friends and I dropped by my uncle's pizza shop, Pizza Roma, in College Park, before heading to Sherwood. I remember arriving and the restaurant was empty. I knew that Friday was a busy day, but luckily, Thursdays were generally not busy. We all sat at the table right near the window and chatted about life. I took a moment for myself as I looked around the table. I took careful note of each of my friends' faces, and I thought, *At this very moment four years ago, I never knew of these individuals' existence, and here I am, years later, with them as my best friends.* I saw flashes of all the great memories we had together and felt a sense of calm overtake me.

We talked about our time together, and one moment in particular that we all had recently been a part of stood out. For Mr. Stelzner's English class, we'd been assigned a creative project where we had to recreate a scene or scenes from any books we had read throughout the year. Putting our heads together, we decided to reimagine William Shakespeare's "Hamlet" set in the world of the Marvel Cinematic Universe, and in particular, *Avengers: Infinity War*. Our plan was simple: have Hamlet and Horatio as our protagonists and Claudius as Thanos. The infinity gauntlet would instead be a sword, given the time period, and the story of Hamlet would be kept the same.

Given our budget limitations and time constraints, we only had one day to film, so we gathered whatever we could and had the whole school as our set. We stumbled across another mutual friend of ours who happened to be roaming the hallways and asked him to be our Thanos, to which he graciously agreed. We mirrored shots to the actual *Avengers: Infinity War* movie but with a Shakespearean twist. It was a day of fun and excitement, and the finished product was perfect, with a blooper reel at the end as the cherry on top. We showed it to Mr. Stelzner and he loved it, along with our classes that got to watch it.

I was reminded by my friends about coming to Blair after private school. "Could you imagine if you went to another high school? You would have never met us," said one of them.

When he said that, something about that statement made me pause for a moment. I lost my ability to speak for a few seconds. It seemed as though that statement summed up my entire life: a collection of moments that could have gone either way but went a specific way and I was just there for the ride. Then it finally hit me. What if all those years ago, I hadn't come to Blair? Everything I experienced in the last four years would never have happened, not to mention the fact that I would never have met anyone I knew now through volleyball.

I didn't want to imagine a life without all the amazing and special people I'd come to know. I didn't want to imagine the person I'd be had I not had all my experiences at Blair. Reflections like those make you think about life in a completely unique way and help you appreciate it more.

We finished up with a discussion about the upcoming game and then headed out.

The drive to Sherwood was a long one, and heavy traffic only added to the time it took to get there. I had "God's Plan" playing on my radio with the volume cranked up as high as my ears could bear. We arrived at Sherwood late. The bus was already parked outside the back entrance, along with all the cars of parents and family members. Everyone was already inside.

I often look back on that day and ask myself if I should have done everything differently. I often dream of it being a perfect day, one where I came on time to the game, left and went back with the team, and did not make the mistake of arriving late to the game. We humans often do this to ourselves where we second guess the past. We think of ways we could have done things differently or wish that certain events had played out a certain way in the hopes it would somehow make life better and perfect. The truth is that there is no such thing. What's happened has happened, and regardless of how we wish it, life will always happen the way it's supposed to.

Like the writing of this book, I wish I had the ability to craft the best possible story in real life. I wish I could make edits and additions in life as I can on my computer screen. I still wonder to this day what the moments leading up to the game were like. I did not arrive on time to walk to the gym along with my team. I didn't get to hear their voices before game time or sense the togetherness of our bond. I didn't get to watch and participate in pregame warmups with my team. I didn't pepper with my cousin, which I had done every game, or look around to see everyone else peppering. I wasn't there for the coin toss and I wasn't there to start the match. I wasn't there to hold a pregame huddle with my teammates and give them words of encouragement like I always did. I felt like such an idiot, and there was no one or nothing to blame but me. God, I wish I had been there for all those things.

Realizing how late I had arrived, I sprinted toward the gym with my clothes and got dressed as fast as I could in the bathroom. I could hear sounds coming from the main gym and echoing in the bathroom. I had no time to notice the details, the trophy case, the fans, the bright colors, or even my own team out on the court. I ran straight to Shio, and I could tell he was not happy with me. He asked if I needed to warm up, which I did in a small room outside the gym. I rushed it, constantly fixated on the game about to come. I heard the whistles and sounds of cheers. The game had already begun and Blair was down by five points (coincidentally just as we had rehearsed it during our previous practice). Shio quickly subbed me in, and I immediately gathered everyone together. "Hey, guys, I'm really sorry about being late, this is all my fault," I started.

Brenna, Jaya, Olivia, Tyler, and Avery looked at me and shook their heads. Bless their souls for supporting me and telling me it wasn't my fault. They had every right, along with the whole team, to be mad and me, yet they still wrapped their arms around me with a smile on their faces and gave me words of encouragement. I knew in my heart I was to blame for how this all started. Realizing I was in the middle of a game, I had to block out any thoughts or emotions and focus on playing volleyball.

We broke the huddle and focused our sights on the incoming serve. Sherwood was holding back nothing. They were attacking every position on the court. Serve receiving was a real challenge, given how each of their servers brought something new. One would utilize a knuckleball, another a floater, and even top spins. Usually, teams have a couple of strong servers, but Sherwood had a full rotation of them. We had trouble with their serves and offensive hitting. On offense we tried our best to get direct kills, but their blocking was enough to slow down our hits, allowing their back row to get easy passes to their setter. They were in control of the whole set. They eased their way to winning the first set as if they were playing against a ghost team.

Armstead and Shio pulled everyone aside and told us to forget the first set. It was back to 0-0 they said. Of course it was hard for us to ignore the fact that we were down 1-0, but they wanted us to keep the game simple and not get caught up with the scoreboard. It was really hard to concentrate, given how loud the Sherwood bleachers were, and because the scoreboard was in our field of vision, we would by default end up catching a glance of the score, each time deflating our confidence. Not to mention the Sherwood side of the court was packed with blue. Our side of the bleachers was not as packed.

We began the second set a little better. We traded some points with them and started to make things a little more competitive. They called timeout and ran some different lineups, which caught us off guard. Bad as it was with their original lineup, we now had to worry about another adjustment. They pulled away with another lead. Their focus and mental strength were reflected in how they played.

On one particular play during the second set, Sherwood sent over a ball that was shanked. I ran across the court and did a bicycle kick pass like I had done one time previously in the season to get the ball back into play. I just remember sprinting full speed and watching the ball go over my head, hoping it would be good enough for a pass or middle hit. The ball flew to Brenna in the middle. She approached to hit it, but their middle was already set and waiting for the block. It seemed like nothing we tried was working. They won the second set, making it 2-0.

At the beginning of the third set, our nerves kicked in full gear. I could sense the fear in everyone's hearts, including my own. Our side was a stark contrast to Sherwood's. Before the set began, I called everyone in for a huddle. In my head I was torn because I knew that third set might be it. It might be the last time we graced any court together as a team. Although we still had a shot, I wanted to say a few words in case I never got to hold another huddle with my team ever again. I looked at everyone in the huddle and just thanked them. I told them how special they were to me and that whatever happened that day, it would never change who we all were to each other, how special our season had been, and how wonderful the experiences we had that year had been. Energized, we headed out for the third set, the most important set of our season.

We started with a great first couple of points. Taking a slight lead, we built some confidence. Our play was starting to gel more and reflect who we had been all season. Sherwood was giving it their all, and their side got louder with every point. We inched our way to make it a close game, down by only a couple of points, with some comeback serves that landed us aces.

Sherwood retook the lead with their strong defense and powerful offensive hitting attack. We fought and tried our best to bring the score to the 20s, but they ultimately pulled away. Just before Sherwood would score the game-winning point, I had a chance to take in the scene. I looked around. I saw everyone sitting along the bleachers, my dad with other parents and my best friends. I saw fans from Blair and then my teammates on the court. I knew this was it, and it absolutely shattered my heart. Sherwood served the last point and went on to win the set and the game, 3-0. The ref whistled to signal the end of the game, and just like that, a journey that had started three years ago was over.

I dropped my head in despair. I didn't want to look up nor did I have the energy to move. We all hugged each other on the court, and I felt comforted in my teammates' arms. Our hug was long and emotional. We didn't have to say a word. Our beating hearts spoke for us, and our souls were uplifted by each other's bright eyes. It was one of those times in your life when you didn't want to leave that comfort because you knew that once you did, it would be gone forever. But we knew we had to move on. With our broken hearts and torn spirits, we jogged to the middle of the court to shake hands with Sherwood. As everyone came around, we gathered in front of our bleachers. I looked over and saw faces that deepened my sadness. I saw some people cry. I looked over at Mr. Fong, Jaya's parents, my dad, and everyone there and felt like I let them all down. It was at that moment that all the negative thoughts began flooding in. The infinite what-if scenarios that never were and never would be. I walked over and hugged everyone.

In our despair we found comfort in each other's arms. It was a heartbreaking defeat, but we had each other and that triumphed anything. I went over to Jaya and Brenna and apologized for how I had played. I felt like it was all my fault, and I began to hate myself immensely. We embraced each other and exchanged words of comfort. They all accepted me with open arms and told me it was no one's fault, that we all were in this together, and that whatever happened was a collective effort.

As I found my way around everyone, my eyes caught Shio in the midst of all the noise and chaotic scenery. From his body language, I knew he was drained and lifeless. His usual smile was not there, and I could see in his eyes that look of defeat. He was the one I felt for the most. After everything he had done for the coed volleyball program and for us, the long hours after school spent coming up with gameplans and lineups, the countless sacrifices he made in his own life to be with us and coach us, the big leap of faith he took to coach a sport no one cared about, and I couldn't give him the conclusion he deserved. I began my volleyball journey with him and I just wanted to see him happy. Winning the county championship would have been something amazing, not just because it would have been the first time in school history but because it would have been the least I could do to repay him for everything he had done for us.

I walked over to the top of the bleachers to meet my friends. They all gave me words of encouragement. I grabbed my gear and looked down at all my teammates. It was as if our sidelines were running in slow motion while Sherwood was beaming with celebrations. Each second more I spent in that gym only caused me more pain. With my broken hopes and dreams, I left the court that day to be haunted by that experience forever.

On our way home, I could not think about anything except the game. My friends tried their best to snap me back into the present, but I was lost in the past. As we passed through the streets, everything I looked at seemed to remind me of the game and, more importantly, my own failures. I turned on the radio in an attempt to drown out my thoughts, but it didn't help. As we continued on, a sudden voice caught my attention. It so happened that the song "Easy" by The Commodores came on. When I heard Lionel Richie's voice, a sense of peace and joy came over me. His words penetrated my heart and eased the pain I was feeling throughout my body. Lionel Ritchie sang with that calm and blissful voice of his.

It transported me back to a time long ago when I was driving home with my dad. It was just the two of us at night on a fairly empty highway. We had a father-son moment while listening to old tracks from my dad's younger days. That same song, "Easy," had come on, and I remember the music just taking us over. The tone and lyrics filled the car with this energy and radiance, and I looked over to see my dad's face brighten at the sound of Lionel Ritchie's voice. The more he smiled, the more I smiled.

That memory instantly snapped me out of my fixation with the Sherwood game. I was transported back to the present and had a similar experience. I glanced to my right and into the rearview mirror to see the blissful faces of my best friends. At that moment we were all lost in the song and we poured our emotions out. It was truly a unique experience and the memory of it always brings a smile to my face. I slowly began to internalize that experience, and my understanding of life grew a little clearer.

Any moment or experience that happens to us in our life isn't the work of an accident. I didn't just happen to join coed volleyball three years prior and just end up losing a semi-final playoff game. It was all part of a specific and outlined journey I was being taken on. Those moments that happen to us happen for a reason, and the more we try to fight them, escape them, or ignore them, the more they won't make sense to us. (And they may even end up hurting us.) Our jobs aren't really to understand them, because, let's be honest, who can really understand it all? What we can do, however, is go along for the ride with a smile on our faces and let the journey take us wherever while enjoying the view, the people, and the beautiful times along the way.

Chapter 30

Ten Letters Spell Volleyball

I arrived home and checked my phone to try to find some way of distracting myself from any thoughts about the game. That would prove impossible, as I knew everyone was having a post-game talk in our group chat. I tried my hardest to not open the chat, but I couldn't resist. If there was one thing that mattered more to me than anything, it was my team.

Noah started off the night with a text that stated, "Not enough God's Plan."

That made me smile a little. I kept scrolling as various players all praised our team and the year we had, and they were right for doing that. We had a great deal to be happy about. If you were to ask someone a year prior whether or not Blair would make it to the semi-final round of the playoffs, they would have more than likely said no, yet there we were.

Because our season and the school year were winding down, we talked about doing some last things together before we went our separate ways. We threw around ideas. There were mentions of sleepovers, pool parties, and such, but Jaya stepped in and wanted to keep it simple. It didn't matter what we did, as long as we were together. Our presence together other far outranked anything. We decided to have one last practice the following Monday then head to Four Corners to grab some food at Chipotle and then more frozen yogurt.

It became emotional at one point when it hit everyone how the seniors were graduating and leaving the team for good. That was always the hardest part about playing sports. Over time you developed a close bond with people who at first you never knew but who, over time, became your best friends. And then, suddenly, it would be over in the blink of an eye. Some of us had spent years together, yet those last couple of weeks in school felt like seconds.

The last day of school for seniors was May 25, 2018, giving us a nice cushion of days to enjoy each other's company and fully soak in the high school experience.

In the middle of it all, I texted everyone and apologized for my "sh*t" play against Sherwood. To be honest, I could have had a perfect stat line and it wouldn't have mattered to me anyway. I wanted the win so badly. I was met with responses of kindness from everyone.

As I sat in my room, having the time of life with my friends, I had a little flashback moment of walking through the main entrance of Blair for the first time as a freshman. The first week leading up to high school had been filled with anxiety and panic. You're probably wondering if it was because of the classes or having no friends, but it wasn't. It was about what I was going to wear. You wear the same outfit for nine years in a private school and all of a sudden you're asked to pick your own outfit. Strange, right? I was worried about fitting in. Would I talk like other people? How would they react to me?

That first day of high school was like being dropped on a foreign planet with no map or script to follow. I didn't know where to go or what to do, it was just a learn-as-I-go kind of experience. I've had an easier time navigating theme parks and cities than high school. It was like learning how to walk again. You feel like you've done it before and you know it, but you're still figuring it out. There were so many rooms, so many floors, and so many people!

I managed to work my way through my first day. As I arrived home, I breathed a sigh of relief. I had felt like an outsider the entire day. I had no friends, no one to talk to, and I felt like I never really fit in.

It got better over time, but things weren't always easy. There were times throughout high school when we all experienced some pretty difficult stuff. Life isn't just about the good stuff. That's the journey we all take in life. Sometimes, you need those bad days to remind you of the good days, and like one of my teachers always said, whenever it's a bad day, just remember the good times because they help you appreciate things more. A cool little trick if you ask me. Maybe that's the whole point of it, you know. Bad days and good days need each other because they help you fully experience the richness of what it means to be a human.

Where had all the time gone, I wondered to myself. Just yesterday I was a freshman and in a couple of weeks I would be graduating and going to college.

I got another notification from Twitter. Our final game was announced all over Blair with Mrs. Johnson and Blair sports retweeting Mr. Fong's initial tweet. "What a ride! What a season! Thanks to ALL the players, Coach Shiotani, and Coach Armstead. Coed finishes 12-2, losing only to Sherwood. One last time through the line!" he wrote on the tweet, with a video of us high-fiving each other down the line one last time at Sherwood.

I couldn't hold back my tears as I texted everyone how sad I was about leaving. It wasn't so much that I would be not playing volleyball at Blair as it was that I was leaving my friends. This team was special to me, each and every one of them. Other players admitted they began crying as well. It was nice that I was going to school just down the road from Blair so I could always visit. My cousin would be playing one more year, and his younger brother would join the program a year later, so I still had a direct connection to coed volleyball.

Another upcoming event was the annual awards ceremony at Blair. It had been started two years prior and was held in the cafeteria, but this year would be the first time it was held in the main auditorium. Ms. Boule wanted to add a little more formality to the event, and the auditorium was fitting for such an occasion. The increased seating capacity and change in scenery also meant that everyone had to be more careful with how they presented themselves (as the whole Blair community would be present). All sports and major higher-ups from the school would be there to celebrate sports across all seasons.

On Friday Noah texted everyone after school about not wearing his equipment. It was a reminder of how there were no more practices, which made me tear up a little. It felt weird not having practice after school. I had made this schedule every day where I would finish my last period, walk to Shio's room to wait for practice, then head to the gym. Now I had nothing to do but enjoy my last days as a high school senior.

We received word that day about Churchill beating Clarskburg, which meant they would see Sherwood for the county championship. I, like everyone, assumed Sherwood would come out victorious, but if our season was an indication of anything, it was to expect the unexpected.

In our alone time, we decided to head to Four Corners anyway, even though our get-together was scheduled for Monday. We just needed to be with each other as much as we could. We all met at Sweet Frog and enjoyed some hours together talking about the season and our upcoming plans in college. It was one of those days when everything was perfect. I didn't want days like those to ever end.

Prior to leaving, Jaya asked if anyone wanted to join her in getting some things for the upcoming prom. We walked to a flower shop just a minute away and flooded the whole store. At first the store employees were a little surprised to see that many people all at once, but Jaya let them know we were all there with her. In the midst of the many beautiful roses and plants that surrounded us, I got lost in the amazement of it all. There were plants of all kinds, and even though they had their differences, something about them being together added to the whole atmosphere of the shop, much like our own team. We were a collection of unique faces, and put together, we created a beautiful forest of people.

Chapter 31

You Will Always Be Above All

On Monday, May 14, 2018, we were reminded of practice after school to the excitement of everyone. It was only for an hour, but it was a nice way to send off the seniors and close out a chapter of our lives in the very room in which we had created countless unforgettable memories during the last couple of years together.

That final practice was hands down the most amazing practice in my time at Blair. It was so goofy and so funny—there was never a dull moment. Everyone was laughing, and we were enjoying ourselves playing the sport we loved. We didn't have to worry about a season or an upcoming game. It was like being a kid all over again, like the first time you held a volleyball in your hand. Every rule we could think of was broken. People attempted jump serves, and Tyler even attempted a no-look, behind-the-back serve. People tried all kinds of positions, and it was an all-around amazing practice.

As we inched toward our final minutes together, Jaya asked to set me one last time before we officially ended it. I had grown very close to her over two years of playing. The setter-hitter relationship is a unique one, and knowing I would never have a chance to receive one of her sets again was heartbreaking. I was holding back my emotions as best as I could. I couldn't even muster the energy to hit a free ball over the net. We tried again and again, but I kept hitting the net. I try to tell myself it was my emotions, but a part of me never wanted to hit that ball over because I knew once that ball made contact with the ground, it would be the last time I would grace the court as a Blair coed volleyball player. I finally gathered myself and focused whatever energy I had left on that one final hit. Jaya set the ball high to the outside, and I remember jumping up in slow motion and making contact with the ball. A second later, everyone heard a loud boom, and then the ball was suddenly on the floor, rolling away. Just like that, it was over.

I went over to Jaya, and we hugged it out before concluding our practice. "I'm really gonna miss you, captain," I whispered to her.

"I'm gonna miss you too, captain," she responded.

Before we left the gym, Shio and Armstead called us over for one last huddle. We all gathered, drowned in our emotions. They too were getting emotional. I didn't know it then but this would be Shio's last year coaching coed volleyball at Blair, which he announced right then in front of us. We all got pretty sad, especially me. I didn't want him to leave after all he had done, but he had earned it. He would go down in history as the first-ever coach to win a division title for Blair coed volleyball. Little did we all know he was also expecting his first child, which was why he had to leave, but he left the door open for a future comeback as a coach.

Armstead started by thanking each and every one of us. She went over her experiences with coed, noting her first time stepping through those gym doors and how she never expected any of what had transpired during her time with coed. She then proceeded to thank each senior individually, along with the whole team.

Armstead coming onto coed was much like most of our stories—all of our stories, in fact. I could still picture seeing her for the first time and then getting to know her more as the years went on. She and Shio were like the perfect coaching blend. Shio was more of a relaxed coach whereas Armstead was more of a floor general. There were times for fun, but she always made us work harder and develop our skills. Without her, we wouldn't have had anyone to drill us with our post-game stats nor would we have had anyone to hold Saturday practices with, which would end up being our saving grace senior year. We gave her and each other a round of applause.

Shio was up next. He took a deep breath and did his best to not let his emotions show, but he failed miserably. "Well, guys, this is it. I just wanted to thank you for an amazing season. Seniors, thank you for everything you guys have done for this program. All the underclassmen, it's up to you guys now to continue the winning tradition. I came to this sport three years ago when Ms. Boule announced coed was looking for a coach. On a whim I decided to give it a try, and it was a great adventure with you all. I am going to miss each and every one of you. Good luck to all of you. Let's get one last Blair on three before we head out!" His eyes were on the brink of a waterfall of tears.

We huddled closely, altogether drenched in sweat and our emotions. Before we broke our huddle, I told everyone how much they meant to me, and we all shared our thoughts. It was really a cool moment, not just being close together physically but also emotionally. We all were in a good place, we had done all we could to build this team, and more than the stats, more than the awards, more than even the spotlights of success, we cherished each other more than anything. Life had given us the opportunity of a lifetime to play the sport we all loved together.

We looked at each other, trying to figure out who would initiate the final Blair on three. We decided that it needed to be a group effort, all for one and one for all. Altogether, we yelled at the top of our lungs, "BLAIR ON THREE. ONE, TWO, THREE, BLAIR!"

After practice ended and the gym was empty, I had a moment to myself as everyone left. I stood in the middle of the floor, just where the net would be, alone in the gym. I looked around and soaked it all in one last time. I could see the past and present meeting each other all around. As I looked at the gym hallway entrance, I saw my younger self walking in for the first time for tryouts during my sophomore year, not knowing if I would even make the team. I could see everything like a timeline laid out in front of me. The beginning struggles of losing to the heights of winning. I saw each and everyone I ever came across because of volleyball.

Tyler was diving for a ball he knew he didn't need to dive for and got injured because of it. Despite his tendency to do things out of the box, he excelled at everything in volleyball and his personality was like a gravitational pull that drew you in the more you got to know him.

Noah was standing in his middle position, completely taking over games and staying calm and cool through it all.

Avery stood far behind the court line to serve with his graceful composure and proceeded to absolutely take over games as an all-around player.

Tiffany was wearing her white shoes, as she always did, staying quiet but bursting with laughter and smiles once she entered the gym as she proceeded to put on a master class of defense and serving.

Brenna walked in with a smile on her face, like always, oozing with positive energy. She always made everyone around her feel special and was a force to be reckoned with in the middle position.

Jaya walked in with an aura unlike any other. She could capture the attention of everyone in the room in a second, a true floor general and outstanding leader.

Olivia was doing another rendition of some new dance she learned, goofing around, beaming with radiance and happiness, not to mention her unmatched skills on the court even as an underclassmen.

My cousin Muhammad was cracking jokes and teasing everyone on the team, making sure we were always having fun and in a good mood. Laughter is one of the most amazing things to experience as a human and he made sure we had plenty of it.

Fiona was sprinting during drills for any pass that came their way. We'd always tell them to call for help, but they were determined, and their effort and dedication outranked anyone on the team.

River was fully energized—as she always was—yelling after every play and giving everyone on the team a boost to play at a high level.

I saw Edward with his quiet hard work and dedication to getting better with each play. He never spoke loudly or much, but when he did he could make everyone around him smile, not to mention his amazing hitting form!

Mizan was our laughing gas. She always knew the kinds of things to say and do to get people to laugh, even when things seemed dull. She was the best left-handed hitter I ever came across.

I saw Sarah, always teasing people and making them smile. She could turn anything into a joke and had joke competitions with my cousin.

I saw Abby as a youthful setter who always brought fresh energy and a much-needed light mood to the team. She worked hard and her play on the court reflected her progress in perfecting her craft as a setter.

Ruben was attempting another soccer trick, as he did constantly, be it during play or outside of it. His athletic skills transcended beyond the sport of volleyball.

I saw Isabelle, somehow, despite her short stature, being the biggest person on the court. Her defensive skills were so good that we had trouble hitting past her. She was a true defensive artist.

Elisabeth was there, encouraging her teammates. She never let anyone feel down and always brought inspiration and hope to the team.

I saw Coach Armstead holding her clipboard and going over our numbers from the previous game. I could even see when she got mad at the referee during one of our games because of a bad call.

I saw Shio walking into the gym for the first time with his bright smile. As he entered, our eyes lit up. Shio would try to do some of our drills, and at times he would fail miserably, but we always had a good laugh about it.

I saw all the practices we had, the tiring ab workouts, the laughs and moments we shared replaying right in front of me. I could hear the screams and chants from the bleachers, and see Shio and Armstead on the sidelines, along with all my teammates.

I began to cry uncontrollably. Every time I wiped my tears, they would replenish and start again. My arms were drenched and my vision was starting to go. I hadn't cried like that in a long time. I gathered myself and took in every detail of the gym. There was a beautiful painting on the gym hallway side. The floor was radiant with wondrous colors. I looked over at the bleachers, knowing I would never see them again from a player's perspective. All the basketball hoops were up on the ceiling. We had to make sure they were up before every practice and game, which took forever to do. I took notice of the lights, the lights which not only lit up our home games but oftentimes blinded us when the ball went straight up in the air.

The gym had a heavenly feel to it. I had been in that gym for the last three years, yet I never noticed those details before. As I finished crying, I smiled at that beautiful home of mine, a place of happiness and joy, and started to walk out. As I reached the door, I turned around one last time, smiled, and left.

We met again at Sweet Frog. Each second with each other was more special than the last. The sun shone, and I could see the rays glow off each of my friends. They were more than my friends, they were my family. How lucky was I to end up in the right place at the right time to meet all those people? It's crazy when I think about it all, but that beautiful mystery to life is what makes it so fun and interesting. You can try to put a pin on it, but how does one calculate the artistic randomness that leads to life? We shared laughs and more cries together. Luckily, the frozen yogurt numbed our emotions. I must have spent a fortune that day ordering the biggest cup I saw and filling it to the brim with sweet chocolate goodness! The cost didn't matter. It was totally worth it.

The team then headed to Chipotle to grab lunch. They all decided to head to a park near the school to enjoy a mini picnic together. I wanted to go, but I had to be home in time for a family event. As I look back on that moment, not going with the team was another one of those times I would forever regret.

Fiona informed us that they had permission to host a final banquet at their house that upcoming Saturday, May 19, 2018.

They created a spreadsheet to see who was bringing what to eat and drink. It was a nice way of keeping it intimate and simple. We didn't have to worry about reservations or wearing something formal. We could be ourselves and talk for as long as we wanted.

On Tuesday Liv informed us that Churchill won the county championship, beating Sherwood to the surprise of all of us. There were two parts to us. One side was comforted knowing Sherwood had lost, but the other side wondered what we could have done differently to be in that game.

We nailed down a good time for everyone to show up at the banquet being hosted at Fiona's house. My cousin and I were fasting, so we wouldn't be able to eat, but I didn't care because the company of everyone was more important to me. Everyone jotted down their potluck dish (which to no one's surprise had zero ounces of healthy food). The party was scheduled from four to nine p.m., but knowing us, it would go on much longer than that.

Chapter 32

Part of the Journey is the End

I was getting ready to go to Fiona's house when I happened to walk by my desk, on which lay our team picture from the day of our division win. I paused in my tracks and stared at it for some minutes. There were messages written all around and decorations by the underclassmen. That picture had been taken not so long ago, yet it felt like ages. It's crazy how time can fly by. I smiled at it and went on my way.

My cousin decided to skip the party because of his fasting, so I went without him. I arrived at Fiona's house, which was set among a plethora of houses with beautiful trees and greenery all around. I parked in front and walked up to the house. I walked past bright green shrubs, and there were birds all around, singing their hymns. The sun's bright light lit up everything. There were shades of yellow and an array of nature surrounding the house.

A girl I initially thought was Fiona was actually their sister, who looked just like them. She escorted me inside the house to where the entire team was. I walked in and was met with a loud greeting and a huge group hug. There was chatting going on, food on the table, Fiona's dog was walking around, and of course, River had to bring a computer to play games. I initially talked with some players in the living room area, and we shared some stories from the season. They all asked where my cousin was, so I phoned him and put him on speaker. He was busy playing video games and received teasing from everyone on the team.

River challenged me to a game of *Super Smash Brothers*, and Avery tagged along. River handed us a loss with ease, and there was no dispute about who was the king of gaming from that point on. I went around talking with everyone, and we all were having a great time together. Seeing their smiles and radiance uplifted my spirits. Although my stomach was empty that day, my soul and heart were nourished beyond their needs.

Some time went by, and we decided to take the party to the back of Fiona's house. They had this room that was open and large enough to fit everyone. There were windows all around so you could see just over the fences and glance at all the amazing trees of the neighborhood. There were sounds of kids playing, cars driving by, and life happening around us.

We sat around close together, telling each other stories and reliving our season. We didn't know where to begin, so we started from the beginning. Brenna and I had been with coed the longest, so we started off the conversation. I talked about my own experiences with coed and how I came to join. Brenna was already part of the Blair volleyball program and also joined coed that year. We talked about our first losing season, and everyone was surprised as to why we stayed on so long, knowing it may never become a winning program.

I mentioned meeting Shio and everyone individually and funny stories like that time during our second year when we had some time between the end of school and the bus arriving for our away game. I had told Shio I would head home to rest up and grab some food. I didn't have a phone at the time nor did I have a ride, so I had to walk back to school. I walked through the gym doors and everyone was furious at me. "Where the hell have you been?" everyone kept asking. People had been trying to call, Shio had asked players to go look for me, emails were sent, and I simply responded, "I don't have a phone". The part I remember vividly was when Liv saw me in the gym hallway and signaled a cross using her hands (which I was confused about but would later learn was because everyone thought I was skipping the game). The whole room burst into laughter when I mentioned that part.

There were some tough times as well. There were days when we lost some close games and it had been difficult to enjoy volleyball or continue working hard, but we persisted, nonetheless. At times people got into arguments with each other, and there were days when the team felt broken during our first two years, but we always found a way back to each other. Volleyball is what kept us together through it all.

Jaya and I brought up the pregame coin toss. We talked about Shio and some funny moments like Joanne's face pass (Joanne was a player on coed who graduated before the 2018 season) and Avery's iconic face pass. We even brought up Tyler's face-plant story. During our playoff game against Sherwood, Tyler dived to dig up a hit and ended up hitting the floor and sliding. My friends had caught the whole thing on video, and rewatching it made everyone burst into tears. After the play, Tyler had looked so lifeless, but at least he'd had the will to go for the ball! We joked that every year something funny was bound to happen during volleyball season which would live on through the years. Tyler's face dive was now added to that collection of stories.

Everyone went around giving each other nicknames and talking about the things they liked best about the season. There was a moment of silence when it hit all of us how our time together was coming to an end. We all got emotional and comforted each other with more funny stories. Hours, which felt like seconds, passed, and I had to depart to go break my fast at another family gathering. Before

I left, the older seniors gave a little pep talk to the underclassmen. We had done all we could for coed, and now they had the responsibility to keep it going. It didn't matter how good or how bad things were, we told them, it was important they never lose sight of the important things: to always trust and love each other, and always give it everything they had and enjoy each and every day they had.

In my heart I knew staying was the right thing to do, but I had to be with my family because I had promised them I would go. As I look back, I wish I had stayed longer. Not a day goes by that I don't regret that decision. I got up to say goodbye, and everyone else stood up right after me. We all got together for one big group hug and held on to each other for a long time. We didn't want to let each other go, but we had to. I thanked everyone personally, especially Jaya. I've always wondered what prompted her to join coed, knowing we only had two wins under Coach Shio our first year, but her joining was one of the biggest reasons we were able to turn things around.

As I drove away, I became overwhelmed with memories of everything from coed. I tried to drown it out with spiritual hymns, slightly increasing the volume each second, but to no effect. I tried to block my emotions and think about other things, but ultimately, all I could think about was that last year of mine. I turned off the radio and rolled the windows down to feel the fresh air. It was a beautiful Saturday evening. The sun was setting and its rays were just piercing the trees. I felt comforted and let the emotions run their course.

The upcoming week after the banquet was our last week as seniors. The awards ceremony was scheduled for Wednesday night. It was going to be a huge night, as the crowd was scheduled to be massive. It was our last official time together as a team, so we had to make it special.

Chapter 33

To You, My Love and Laughter

On Wednesday, May 23, 2018, I went about my day in school with each passing second increasing my anticipation of the awards ceremony. When I got home, I quickly rushed to change, having already picked out my outfit the night before in my extreme excitement. I had kept it casual in previous years, but my senior year was special, so I went with a suit-inspired look but without a button-down and tie, replacing the shirt with a white T-shirt for a summer-inspired look. It was not too formal and fit the mood of the event perfectly.

My cousin and I arrived at the Blair parking lot to find it packed with cars from the front all the way to the end. I had never seen it that packed before. We walked into the main auditorium to find it crowded with students, staff, and parents. There were hundreds of people, all dressed in their unique attire, each with a unique story, under this one roof ours.

The coed and boys' volleyball teams gathered in the seating area on the right. The auditorium was set up in a trio of seating arrangements. As you entered, the main stage was directly in front of you, with three collections of seats separated by aisles, each starting at the main stage and working its way to the entrance/exit doors. I arrived to find most of the team already there and most were dressed up. Of course, Noah was wearing shorts, a total Noah move. If there was anyone who had the looks and swagger to pull off shorts during a formal event, it was Noah. We all talked before the event started and couldn't stop our giggles in anticipation of our turn to go up on stage.

Shio walked over and greeted all of us, along with Ms. Armstead and Coach Chris from boys' varsity. Coach Chris came over to me and whispered, "I'm still mad at you for stealing away Avery and Tyler from boys." We shared a laugh.

As time went by, more people joined the auditorium. As the time to start the program grew near, the lights dimmed and various speakers presented themselves. Mrs. Johnson started with an opening monologue thanking everyone for coming and thanking all the athletes and coaches, as well as parents, for an amazing year.

One by one we watched as each varsity sport was called up in order of their respective season. With every sport, the room erupted each time, with friends calling out to their fellow classmates on stage or to the sounds of laughter and giggles. The program came to spring sports and our excitement increased. We were getting very nervous, and everyone was discussing who would go up and in what order.

Finally, they announced, "Up next is coed volleyball." We all shot out of our chairs and headed on stage. Fiona was first, followed by Jaya, Brenna, Isabelle, River, Ruben, Abby, Avery, Muhammad, Mizan, Sarah, me, Tyler, and Noah. Nervously making our way up the stage steps, we tried our best to control our anxiousness. Coed volleyball, which always had the image of a joke sport, was about to change on that very night.

As we gathered, Shiotani and Armstead were already up there waiting for us. They held awards in their hands, but we didn't know who was getting what. They had our team season stats up on a big projected image next to our team photo taken after the division championship game. Of all the sports that year, we'd had one of the best seasons at Blair by far.

The announcer started, "So first of all, the coaches. Coed volleyball is co-coached by Jacquie Armstead and Elliott Shiotani." Everyone gave a light round of applause. He continued, "This year's Blazers were the 2018 division champs for the first time in school history!"

The entire room erupted with cheers and claps. I couldn't stop smiling. I was just so happy that we finally did it, we had brought a title to coed volleyball! The announcer switched the slide to announce the awards for the season. The up-and-coming award was won by Mizan. The coach's award was given to both Fiona and Avery. Tyler won defensive MVP and I won offensive MVP. I must be honest in that I didn't feel comfortable accepting that trophy (or any of my previous ones). I never liked being singled out for something. The entire team was the reason we had a great season. Everyone contributed something, and without each other, we would not have been able to accomplish a regular season 10-1 record.

Shio and Armstead had also informed us that we had ended up breaking every record for coed volleyball there was to break. We held the record for the best record/most games won, the first ever 5-0 division record, the longest winning streak, most sets won, and most points, aces, and kills by a coed volleyball team, not to mention we reset every defensive statistical category as well. We walked off the stage together, proud of having represented and played for Blair coed volleyball.

Along with everyone else, I stayed and watched the ceremony until it finished. It was a great show of celebration and a nice way to conclude our athletic journeys in high school. I always loved those kinds of things, not so much the awards and trophies but the togetherness of an event that celebrated the countless journeys of a group of people. Each of us had a unique story to tell, be it a student or a teacher, yet through all of it, we were able to share a moment of unity despite anything that occurred, be it winning or losing.

Coed at the 2017-2018 sports awards ceremony.

There was a segment during the ceremony when a slideshow showcasing all the sports at Blair was played. There were photos of the team, and a small video showing them playing. When coed was shown, we all screamed, although we were not as loud as track, who happened to have a roster bigger than most sports combined.

The ceremony ended and the lights came back on. We all wiped our tears and applauded everyone involved in sports that year. We hugged each other and talked for a while before leaving.

When I got home I went straight to my room and locked my award inside my closet. Not only was it something I didn't want, as being singled out for an award is never truly something to be happy about, but it reminded me too much of my failures at the Sherwood game. I rested on my bed, thinking about my entire life up to that point. I had two days left in my high school journey, and after that I would no longer be a student at Montgomery Blair High School. More importantly, I would no longer get to play volleyball with my family at Blair.

It was a tough last week for me. I found it hard to sleep at times as I was plagued by constant reminders and nightmares of our loss. There were times when I awoke to the false hopes of beating Sherwood, only to find it was a dream, but it was comforting to know that we had given volleyball everything we had. Although it didn't end the way I wanted it to end, I was just happy to be a part of it all.

CHAPTER 34

Forever in My Heart, Thank You, My Best Friend

On Thursday, May 24, 2018, I went to school with my yearbook. I found my way around each hallway, looking for everyone I had made some sort of connection with to ask for their signatures. It was a day of meeting old friends and reminiscing about old memories. I felt like a freshman again as I soaked in the experience of being a Blazer. As I made my way around, I took notice of each detail that had been hidden from me for the past four years. I walked down Blair Boulevard—the primary hallway in the school—and took notice of everything along its stretched-out route. I had walked that route for four years, yet I had never stopped to truly soak in the details. I took notice of the array of flags representing various countries around the world that hung just above our heads. I saw the senior courtyard that, funny enough, I had never actually sat in. I went to every classroom I had a course in and met all my old teachers. I went back to the main gym, a place I considered my second home, and marveled at its beauty.

Time has a weird way of working. It's always moving linearly, yet sometimes it feels like it stops and reverses. That place I called home was now going to be a distant memory of mine. We all were going to move on, never to see each other again nor have that same feeling walking through those doors early in the morning. There would be no more worries about AP tests or SATs, no more Friday Night Lights, and no more volleyball.

I tried my best to find everyone I could, but there were too many. It was getting late, so I decided to drive home. The student parking lot was at the main entrance of Blair. As I exited the campus, to my right I could see the football stadium, along with the softball and baseball fields. I was going to miss this place. Friday would be our last day. I still couldn't believe it. We were about to graduate high school!

—⚌—

I awoke Friday morning as I always did. I was the only one up in the house. It was a very quiet morning. The sun was just coming up, and you could barely see its glow of yellow, red, and orange behind the trees. The whole neighborhood began to shine with a beautiful gold color. I got into my car and drove to school. Because I lived so close to Blair, it was only about a five-minute drive, but that Friday I took my time. I rolled down the windows to feel the air and decided not to turn on the radio for once. I wanted to fully take in the experience and be in the moment.

There weren't that many cars in the parking lot when I arrived. Instead of walking to class, I sat outside on my car hood, just gazing at Blair. I started to get a little emotional as I recalled how I'd often think about this day as a freshman. My cousins who went to Blair before me all told me how quickly high school would go by. Of course I didn't believe them because back then I had four years in front of me as a Blazer, but now I only had eight hours left.

Each class was more painful than the previous one. It was an all-period day, giving us one last goodbye to all of our teachers. I got to see all my old teachers at Blair and thanked them for everything. I got to see all my teammates and friends I had come to know over the years. With each handshake and gentle hug, I was constantly reminded of the infinitely beautiful experiences I'd had.

I didn't realize it at the time, but what one remembers most about meaningful experiences is not primarily the experiences themselves but the special people who are tied to those experiences. In my time at Blair I was lucky enough to meet friends, teachers, mentors, and coaches who inspired me to be kind, taught me about the important things in life, gave me inspiration and hope, and helped me learn, develop, and grow. And beyond that, they showered me with the gifts that make life purposeful and meaningful. My love for life and all its wonders increased tenfold. I will forever be in debt to all the beautiful souls I had the pleasure of meeting during my time at Blair.

I remember one experience vividly from that day. I walked into my sociology class to thank and say goodbye to Mr. Smith, the teacher. When I entered the room, Jaya happened to be there. We both had the same class with him and often talked to each other before and after the coed season. I remember seeing her there and not saying anything. I walked over to her and we embraced in a long hug. No words were said, we just let our emotions speak for us. I had my eyes closed because I knew the moment I opened them I would break down. It was probably very awkward for Mr. Smith, but he let us have the time because he also knew how special it was. This was our last goodbye. I got so lost in my sadness that I almost forgot about Mr. Smith. We finally snapped out of our senses and said goodbye. I said goodbye to some other people and got some last-minute signatures from the volleyball team, and just like that, it was over.

—⁂—

Graduation was held at the University of Maryland in College Park, Maryland, on Tuesday, June 5, 2018. It was a surreal moment because it felt strange how one moment you were a freshman on your first day of school and, in the blink of an eye, you were now graduating high school. I picked up my friends and we drove over early, arriving on a beautiful sunlit campus. I met up with some old friends and teammates. I saw Mr. Fong, Tyler's dad, there, and it took me back to all those moments at our games when I looked over my shoulder and saw him on the bleachers, cheering us on.

We sat through a series of speeches by various speakers. Xfinity Center was filled with parents, family members, and friends who cheered us on. At the end of the speeches and ceremony, we all rose together, turning our tassels and officially attaining the status of graduates. As we were dismissed, over 800 students flooded toward the exits. I myself got lost in a sea of red and white. I would see hints of people I knew then my vision would be disrupted by the sight of unfamiliar faces.

As we exited Xfinity Center, I was blinded for a moment by the sun's rays. Parents and family awaited as we exited. I met up with my family. We embraced and took what felt like a thousand pictures. I looked around and saw the faces of hundreds lit up by smiles and moments of joy. I was lucky enough to find Jaya wandering around. We hugged and said our goodbyes to each other. I tried my best to look for Tyler, Avery, Tiffany, Brenna, and Noah, but I couldn't find them. Part of me will forever regret not seeing them one last time, but another part of me was comforted, knowing it would have been too emotional for me.

I drove home along with my cousin with the biggest smile on my face. When I arrived I immediately changed out of my graduation gown and sat down in a meditative state, closing my eyes, and feeling an immense sense of peace and gratitude overtaking me. I didn't want to think about anything, I just wanted to feel the essence of life and reflect on another chapter of my life that had closed.

I think about those years of my life every day. It was a time of happiness and mystery, a time when I didn't know what the future would be. I still have that Wilson volleyball. When I look at it and hold it in my arms, I often think how lucky I was to come across the sport of volleyball all those years ago. Volleyball, beyond any other sport, gave me a love for life. I found myself at the heart of a wonderful place with amazing people. I met Shio through volleyball, I had all those memorable experiences with my friends, and it made me who I am today.

Volleyball is so much more than a sport; it's a way of life. And to be honest, the game never truly ends. It will always be a part of me and will continue to teach and inspire me in ways I could never imagine.

As the years went by and I got a little older, I began to understand more and more about life and all of its mysteries. When we are all young, we sometimes get lost in our fun, and that's totally okay. Maybe that's the whole point of it all. When you're young, you don't worry about too many things, but as you get older, your understanding of everything becomes clearer. I don't know why my life played out this way, or what the grander-than-life reasons are behind its trajectory. If you were to ask me as a kid if I could imagine myself falling in love with a sport called volleyball and going on an adventure of a lifetime, I would have said no for sure. The truth is, I wouldn't have wanted it to play out any other way. (Well, I probably would have wanted to win counties, though.)

After I graduated high school, I would go back to watch all the home games at Blair. My cousin was a starter and was even elected captain. It had been cool to see him grow along with me, and now he was captaining the program just as us seniors had wanted the underclassmen to do. The underclassmen had all come into their own and were now the core of the team. It was nice being able to see my cousin and his brother play. I imagine that's what it feels like watching kids grow right in front of your eyes.

Sometimes, Shio and some older players like Brenna would be there, and we would sit and talk for hours about the new team and the good old days. Blair even made the playoffs again, making it a first in history to go three years in a row with a playoff appearance. Ms. Boule would also drop by the games and was happy when she saw us.

We do our best to get together at least once a year at the same center that Fiona rented where we had our pre-season tryouts before my senior year. Everyone talks about their post-graduation experiences, we get to play together, and it's also fun watching the newcomers learn and grow.

Not a day goes by where I don't think about volleyball or my experience with it at Blair. I am one of those people who thinks that everything in life happens for a reason. I sometimes question why I was lucky enough to have those experiences, but the truth of the matter is that life is full of those types of rich experiences. We sometimes let those rare bad times get to us, and we can get lost in those things, but at the end of the day, they never compare to how good life can be. And when it's good, it's really good! Volleyball just makes me so happy.

I have always had this thought in my mind about doing something to say thank you to volleyball and, more importantly, to all the special people in my circle at Blair, but I could never find something that felt right. I was lucky enough to come across inspiration from a book by Kathy Bresnahan called *The Miracle Season* and decided to write a book titled *Dear Volleyball*. It is not much, but it is the least I could do for the sport that changed my life.

To whoever you are who is reading this, wherever you are, and whenever you are, I'm hoping that as you play this experience back, it's in celebration of your own beautiful journey in life as well!

Chapter 35

Dear Volleyball

Dear Volleyball

Where do I even begin?
It was love at first sight
Our first time a no-win
The second, not so bright
My time with you changed me
I was given a family
Moments that made me happy
Crouched and ready I wait desperately
My heart fully committed to you
I'm so happy when I'm on the court
The feeling I get is always new
Like the opening of a story, so very short
One can only dream
All we've been through
The sweeps so clean
The hard-earned dues
In the end, you kept me going
My heart and soul continually growing
From watching you on the sidelines
Dreaming of victory

Dear Volleyball

To holding up a trophy of a lifetime

Making history

I never wanted it to end

Times of joy and happiness

The beautiful moments with friends

Isn't it so sweet?

The next one after

I can't believe we're here

At the end of a chapter

Ten letters spell volleyball

You will always be above all

Part of the journey is the end

To you, my love and laughter

Forever in my heart, thank you, my best friend

2017-2018 Montgomery Blair High School Coed Volleyball Roster

#1 AbdulAziz Baig	OH/LB	Senior
#3 Muhammad Niyaz Baig	LB	Junior
#4 River Rohrman	OH	Junior
#5 Avery Liou	RH/RB	Senior
#6 Tyler Fong	MB/MH	Senior
#7 Isabelle Megosh	MB	Freshman
#8 Mizan Arum	MH	Freshman
#9 Abby Brier	RB/S	Freshman
#10 Elisabeth Jang	RB/LB	Sophomore
#11 Brenna Levitan	MH	Senior
#12 Jaya Hinton	S	Senior
#13 Fiona Haverland	S	Junior
#14/2 Tiffany Mao	MB/L	Senior
#15 Edward Lin	RH/MH	Sophomore
#16 Olivia Freer	OH	Sophomore
#17 Sarah Kapstein O'Brien	MH	Freshman
#25 Ruben Moulton-Huber	RB	Freshman
#27 Noah Kim	MH	Senior
Elliott Shiotani		Head Coach
Jacqueline Armstead-Thomas		Assistant Coach

www.ingramcontent.com/pod-product-compliance
Lightning Source LLC
Chambersburg PA
CBHW061206070526
44583CB00025B/3132